PLUCKY COUNTRY

We should lead the world ... again

Author: Geoff Stewart

Publisher: Geoff Stewart

Dedication

*There are many people in my personal diaspora, from the
transatlantic yachting community, to business people in
London, the computer community, arbitrators, professional
associations, sporting clubs, village cricketers, academic
colleagues, students, family and social connections.
Forgive me for not personally acknowledging everyone, there
are thousands.
Everyone had a story to tell. I have learnt something from
everyone I have met and I am grateful for both the information
and the entertainment.
The carnival of life is endlessly engaging.
Clearly, I need to get out more and meet some more people.
May I apologise for the preponderance of Victorian examples
in this text. My knowledge of who is doing what, with which
and to whom in Peppermint Grove, Rundle Street, Huonville, on
Coochiemudlo, the Tiwi Islands and the Rocks needs expanding.
This book is also dedicated to all the Plucky
Aussies, past, present and future who create and
operate the wonderful world we live in.*

COVER IMAGE

Trevor Piercy tending to CSIRAC one of the first computers in the world built in Australia to Australian design with all components built in Australia.

MOJO

Plucky Aussies

We Plucky Aussies can have a glorious future.

We have led the world in harvesters, computers, centrifuges, giving women the vote, black box flight recorders, WiFi, Australian Crawl, yachting, hydro electricity, Aluminuim Ships and much more.

We also have Gold, Aluminium, Uranium, Lithium, Rutile, Silver, Tin, Lead, Zinc, Copper, Drones, Simulation and Swarm Technology.

We have been here before.

In 1880 we had the highest standard of living in the world, an open free and happy society.

It is time to get our MOJO back, 'cmon Aussie cmon'.

Take Back Control

This is a manifesto for the restoration of control of Australian society to the mainstream Aussies who do the work and pay for the health, schooling, welfare, military, customs, baristas and everything else.

Donald Horne in 'The Lucky Country' suggests that our prosperity is an accident.

Not so, Aussies have led the world in many domains and deserve a great life.

We have the people, the resources and the pluck to restore the open, free, happy, productive and fulfilling life we once had.

Mr. T.

Tolstoy in Anna Karenina gave us 'happy in the same way and unhappy in their own particular way', we flip this for Australia to 'happy in their own individual way and sad in the standard plucked way', whingeing about some foreign, confected, apocalyptic, university proselytised nonsense.

I'm Alright Jack

The old elite in Australia, like Tsar Nicholas in Russia, have been asleep at the stick, or is it schtick, comfortably, casually cruising along - gin and tonic in hand - believing that 'I'm alright Jack' was an everlasting strategy. Meanwhile the new whingeing class have taken control. It is self-harm on the scale of the 1917 Russian capitulation. They are coming for you.

Productive People

Australia is full of Plucky Aussies who keep the world turning every day. Not only do we do useful work, we collaborate, cooperate and negotiate the everyday interactions that enable life to flourish.
We are the people who will create our glorious future.

Structure

In the pages that follow we will:
- consider industries which might support our future
- examine our institutions to see if they are fit for purpose
- propose some fiscal responsibility
- tell some Plucky Aussie people stories.

We hope that you enjoy the celebration of the vast achievement of Plucky Aussies and that you will engage in the restoration of freedom to the productive citizens of our wonderful country.

My fellow Plucky Aussies, it is up to us.

GENERATING WEALTH

Best In The World

Australia has led the world in a number of industries and can lead the world in several more. As mentioned above, the list includes mining software, winemaking techniques, design and construction of harvesters, spooling software, WiFi, aluminium ferries, ulcer treatment, std prevention, immunology, rust free wheat, feminist writing, film making, yacht design, military strategy, trajectory sensing technology, military vehicles, rock music, digeridoos, woomeras, fire-stick farming, sheep breeding, ice-making, stump-jump plough, pharmacology, poetry, black-box flight recording, wine making, computer design and construction, wine packaging, climate research, bionic ear technology, geoscience and aerial crop spraying.

Not bad for a small country. If you were not accustomed to thinking of Australia as a country that has led the world, please come up to date.

This list could have come from Leporello in Don Giovanni.

Opera schmopera, what about the future?

Future Leadership

Australia can lead the world in the Aluminium, Nuclear, Hydrogen, Ferries, Rail technology, Electricity production industries and more.

Let me repeat 'lead the world'. No more forelock-tugging, branch office obedience and colonial cringe.

Many seemingly important Aussies have just been cringers,

because it is easier to obey instructions than think. 'All the way with LBJ', 'fully vaccinated' and 'net zero by 2050' come to mind.

Maybe these politicians are accustomed to following the direction of lobbyists and sponsors and are incapable of independent thought. That is why the lobbyists put these ciphers in place.

We need people in parliament and in the media who will pursue the best interests of Australia, not just recite fashionable, foreign clichés.

Qantas Strokes Itself

In 2008 Qantas should have purchased multiple other airlines as the Australian economy was sustained by trade with China and the rest of the world was belly-up. What did they actually do? Congratulate themselves on how clever they were to survive the GFC. Another large opportunity not exactly missed, it was not even noticed.

Insight And Courage

Why does it make sense to allow overseas interests to control of Australian opportunities? Do Americans buy our real assets with fake QE dollars?

The challenge for us is to have the courage to build major Australian businesses. Are our bankers, investors, insurance companies and regulators on board with this project? Do they care?

Well, they care about a fat, lazy, easy life for themselves. That is NO.

We need to replace these self-serving ciphers with people who have the courage and insight required to help Australia grow and flourish.

Wombat Whisperer

We will need a new generation of directors, the current cabal are more concerned about their own comfort and wombats than the future of Australia. Hundreds of Thousands of dollars a year to go to 10 meetings. Some of them do not even read the briefing papers, let alone contribute to the discussion.

Not clear what the 'Wombat Whisperer' is doing in this club.

Brazen Bozo Bankers

Macquarie is world class, however the big 4 banks spent most of their time as lazy, oversize building societies, with large spreads on mortgage funding. They stole the savings of the trusting, pre-war generation with low interest rates.

Listen up you puffed up, fat, lazy arrogant bankers, you should not be proud of stealing the savings of trusting little old ladies. It is time to lose the strut and earn your place.

Sharing The Fruits

In early 20th century Australia, imports were taxed to facilitate the development of local manufacturing and to allow the payment of inflated wages to workers. This policy spreads the benefits of industry more widely and allows many people to enjoy the freedom that comes with prosperity.

However, the problem is that cosseted manufacturing is not internationally competitive. When the tariffs were reduced in the 1970s, many manufacturers folded and many high wage jobs were lost. Manufacturing went from 26% of the economy to less than 10%.

Do our current policy settings help to build a society with wide levels of cooperation, low levels of disputation and a widely shared prosperity?

Our prosperity derives from advances in science and technology. Did the 1% create our prosperous world? Did they invent the internet? No and No. Did they invent the wheel, the use of fire, electricity, computers, aluminium, simulation, cooking, the domestication of yeast and much more? I think not.

They are parasites who have managed to divert the dollars - earnt by others - into their own dachas.

How does it make sense to give the prizes to people who did not run in the race, but merely manipulated the results.

Projects

ARPA and DARPA were government funded projects in America that led to the internet. Teflon came from space research. CSIRO created WiFi, we need many more such projects.

The Snowy Mountains Hydro-electricity project delivered irrigation, flood mitigation, dispatchable, low cost electricity, many jobs and the development of a valuable set of skills and knowledge. The Snowy people still provide consulting advice to hydro-electricity projects around the world.

Race, Rain And Rape

Race, rain and rape are the three 'Rs' currently proselytised in our pseudo universities (selective [in the name of diversity], lefty, zealot whinge clubs). Was there a time when universities sought to generate and transmit knowledge?

We must get rid of the plague of managerialist administrators and the ideologues in the academic staff. Time to start some new institutions with a desire to discover new knowledge and help young people to learn and grow.

What about having professorships devoted the the aluminium or the nuclear industries in our new institutions. We must find ways to start again and get some value.

Knowledge, Truth And Learning

In breaking news: The University of Austin has just been created to pursue knowledge, truth and learning, free from the woke drivel that is endemic in contemporary tertiary academe. Time for Aussies to create new institutions where our children can get an education.

Chips

The world needs a reliable source of computer chips. We could do it. Perhaps we might start with some joint ventures with the chip makers in Taiwan. Alternatively we could purchase an entire working chip making plant from Japan or the US. That was how Taiwan got started.

We need some politicians and managers who can see these opportunities and make things happen.

Kiss A Miner

Our miners (two of the top three in the world) have developed world leading mining approaches, infrastructure, software and processes to lead the world. This success pays for the lifestyle of the ignorant and arrogant city slickers.

Is this taught in school, that the bush pays for the lifestyle in the cities? Do we celebrate the achievements of our miners? Do we have 'kiss a miner' day?

No, instead we have preaching by the poly-gendered publicists about their preferred pronouns. Should we send the alphabet soup people to work in the mines? Too late, the mines are automated already. What are we to do with this rainbow parade of recalcitrants? Get them out of the media would be a good start. That a tiny group of people want to give themselves funny names is not mainstream news.

There have always been cults with their own terminology. Remember the 'Dead Poets Society'?

Reserves

The good news is that we have vast reserves of iron ore (52 billion tonnes), bauxite (9,8833 million tonnes), uranium (one third of the world total), copper (84 million tonnes), coal (30,000 million tonnes), Gold (2,966 tonnes), Diamonds (9.69 million Carats), Lead (9.15 million tonnes), Gas (70 trillion cubic feet), plus much more, Antimony, Lithium, Manganese, Mineral Sands, Nickel, Rare Earths, Silver, Tin and Zinc.

Currently we have a world class mining industry digging this stuff up and sending it overseas. We have been discussing since the 1960s the desirability of turning these materials into cars, cameras and computers and exporting elaborately transformed items rather than just the raw materials. It is a great idea now it is time to get on with it.

Schmoozers, Slitherers And Swindlers

We will need capable politicians and managers, we have strong candidates, however the current pre-selection process had been captured by special interest groups so we will need a fresh approach.

No more schmoozers, slitherers and swindlers, we seek people with courage, conviction and commitment.

Courage, Conviction And Commitment

Get the right people in place, then we can lead the world. Head Office, not branch office. In America, the Chief Marketing Officer becomes the Managing Director. In Australia the Chief Accountant is appointed to be the Managing Director. Why the difference?

Australia is dominated by lazy oligopolies where administering the cash flow is all that is required. Creating an International Business is not even considered.

Our bankers, insurance companies and superannuation funds between them control 40% of the investment in the Australian Stock Exchange. Are they a force for good? Do they invest in industry leading projects? Export projects? Should we allow them to continue to transfer 30% of superannuation 'investments' into their own pockets as fees?

Do they find 'branch office' style investments to be simpler and easier. Some of them just pleasure themselves with woke whimsy. Who are they accountable to? Do they exercise their power to advance the future of Australian? They pay themselves fat salaries, but do not explore the opportunities or take the risks for which they are paid.

This is demonstrated by the decline in the ANZ share price when they sacked John McFarlane and hired Mike Smith to pursue growth in Asia. 'Hats off' to Charles Goode and his board who had the courage and foresight to pursue international opportunities.

Recommendation: Dismantle the corrupt superannuation industry and allow citizens to invest for their own future.

Real Engineers Not Social 'Engineers'

Meanwhile our truly stupid politicians paid billions of dollars to delay the exit of international car companies. Kept a couple of jobs for a couple of years, the usual brainless short- term, politician inspired band-aid.

Parliament should be considering high impact national issues, not arrogant, impertinent and ineffective social engineering. Who gives a toss about 'gay liaisons/moments', whatever that is? The pronoun pedants, should push off.

Lightly-Bearded Lothario

In the 1970s at speaker's corner in London, a lithe, lonely, lightly-bearded lothario, looking lovely on a soap box was advocating gay marriage. I asked him why when many were trying to get out of marriage, he wanted to get in. I am still waiting for an answer. Is it access to superannuation?

Export Or Die

Exporters generate the funds required to pay for cars, cameras, computers, mobile phones, Thai prawns, Californian oranges, cosmetics, medicines, petrol and all other imports.

City dwellers in Australia neither earn nor deserve their standard of living. What do they export? We should ensure that all Aussies understand this and that our export industries are both recognised and very well supported.

Recommendation: Materials should be developed to enable all Aussies to understand that exporters pay for the standard of living we all enjoy.

In the following pages we consider some industries that can have a substantial influence on Australia's future. We hope to ignite some discussion that will produce the policies and investment required for Australia to take a world leading position in more industries.

ALUMINIUM

Downstream Action

This section asks if the well developed Aluminium industry in Australia might embrace more downstream action, delivering elaborately transformed items to the world, ferries, aeroplanes, iPhone cases and more. The end-use of Aluminium products by sector are as follows: transport, construction, machinery and equipment, electrical, foil stock, packaging, must be some opportunities in there for Plucky Aussies.

Aussies can and should occupy the leadership position in everything to do with aluminium.

Low-cost electricity is essential. See the Nuclear section.

Apple Antics

Steve Jobs when the iPhone 5 was designed to be buried in a block of Aluminium, approached the US Aluminium Industry - which had been manufacturing low precision window frames and car braking systems - seeking high precision drilling. He found that the incumbents were happy to continue their current practices and did not know, and could not be bothered finding out, how to drill with the precision required to provide the case for the iPhone. Jobs went to China to find engineers who were interested to solve the problem. There were thousands of them and they got onto it immediately.

Mines, Refineries, Smelters

Australian has had an Aluminium Industry since 1955, and over the decades it has been a significant contributor to the Australian economy. We have 5 Bauxite mines, 6 Alumina refineries, 4 Aluminium smelters. Our bauxite production is the largest in the world, half exported and half turned into alumina. We are the largest exporter of alumina. With production of aluminium metal, we come in at number 6.

The Bell Bay Smelter in Tasmania was located to take advantage of hydro-electricity, Point Henry in Victoria with a coal mine and generating plant in Anglesea, Portland in Victoria had a special deal to use electricity from the vast reserves of brown coal at Yallourn (enough for 400 years). Wiepa has used traditional generating sets and is now expanding the use of solar.

Long-Term Commitments Required

Mining and smelting require long-term commitments, we must make sure that we provide a long-term, guaranteed supply of low-cost electricity. Australian governments are instead moving to expensive, intermittent electricity. Does this self-harm seem absurd to you?

The Aluminium Industry employs 17,000 people and earns an export income greater than $13 billion. This is admirable.

The question is, what do we have to do to generate more downstream action?

Just Ask

My dream is that anyone in the world who considered using an aluminium component, sub-assembly or product could find in Australia the 'best in the world' advice, design, manufacturing and logistics.

We have been discussing this idea of exporting elaborately transformed products rather than raw materials for many decades. In fact McKay exported harvesters in 1890, Australian wines have been pleasing palates across the world for more than 100 years, Jeff Kennet bought a woollen goods manufacturer in Wangaratta seeking to turn our wool into items of much greater value, Toyota exported Camrys to the Middle East, Boyd Munro in the sixties created Aussie software that changed the world, Austal makes and exports 'best in the world' ferries and military craft and we exported aluminium braking systems to the US car industry.

Big Banana

We can be the big banana in the Aluminium industry for the world. If we could get the clowns in Canberra to grow up and help Australia flourish, rather than twitching to the tune of foreign fools fulminating fantasies about the unknowable climate in 30 years time, or how many genders there are, the mystical meaning of diversity, inclusion, sustainability, equity and other such rent-seeking nonsense, we could make some progress.

Back to Aluminium, we should consult the existing players and industry associations to ask for their assistance on this mission. First we must support the existing businesses with resources and people. Tell us what you need. I promise that we will make commitments to long-term, low-cost electricity.

Next we should consider how to prepare a proposal for more downstream action. Do we put an institution focussed on Aluminium in Weipa? Do we need to allocate land for factories, ports and learning institutions?

Dishonest Universities

A profound dishonesty by current universities is the assertion that the teaching is done by the people who are at the leading edge of research. It is not true. Researchers get teaching exemptions so that they can research more. We should accept this reality.

In the institutions that replace universities, there should be some focussed on research and entirely separate institutions focussed on learning and teaching.

Aluminium Advocacy

May I suggest that the aluminium people have a look at the Finkel, Twiggy hydrogen proposal, it is very persuasive.
The opportunity is there, let us see what can be done.
Oh, and one more thing, aluminium is infinitely recyclable.

NUCLEAR

Jervis Bay Nuclear Plant

Plucky Aussies in 1958 built the first nuclear reactor in the southern hemisphere as a step towards nuclear-based electricity. Land was allocated at Jervis Bay for a nuclear power generation plant and steelworks. Billy McMahon killed the project. One more brainless political decision that inflicted substantial damage on Australia.
We could have been and should have been leaders in the use of nuclear power to generate electricity.
We still can be.

Call And We Will Come Running

Imagine that anyone, anywhere in the world who needed electricity could call an Australian number, declare how much electricity they wanted and that we would design and build the reactor, or supply one off the shelf, supply the raw material, take away the waste, train the locals in how to operate the reactor and power generation assets and consult on any other relevant matter.
Hotel construction and infrastructure projects work in this manner 'BOOT' build, own, operate, transfer. We can apply it to nuclear projects.
Imagine also that the Australian government shared the risk. Trade payment guarantee as in UK. Litigation support where required.

Fukushima

In the 100 years before the Fukushima incident there had been two tsunamis higher than the wall. The disaster should have been foreseen and led to a higher wall or a higher location for the reactor. Instead, they took the easy option and put the reactor close to the water. The disaster was created by incompetence and was inevitable. No 'black swan' here.

The reactors were old and should have been decommissioned (it was planned, however greed at TEPCO kept the old stuff working), 1964 Westinghouse design with the control room in the basement, so that when flooding occurs, the reactors are out of control and blow, a disaster waiting to happen.

Frothing About The War

Instead of understanding the situation and moving on, we had a bout of hysteria. Is there a possibility of getting control of the powerful emotions coming from the brain stem? Hysteria attracts clicks, so the self interested cynics in the media exploit it.

It was ever so, in the run up to the First World War, the Beaverbrook and Northcliffe Press were frothing about war and selling lots of papers.

Currently the 'nudge unit' manipulators can spray fear into the air, then drive the mob wherever they want. Why have a prefrontal cortex if we don't use it? Well, we actually use the smart bit of the brain to explain to ourselves and the world why we did the dumb things coming from the brain stem. Isn't this a delicious paradox. Are you listening Brittany?

We must do better.

Some Facts

Your newspapers should have told you that:

Nuclear energy now provides about 10% of the world's electricity from about 440 power reactors.

Nuclear is the world's second largest source of low-carbon power (29% of the total in 2018).

Over 50 countries utilise nuclear energy in about 220 research reactors. In addition to research, these reactors are used for the production of medical and industrial isotopes, as well as for training.

Voodoo

Who has responsibility for getting these facts on the table? Allowing the 'voodoo' prohibition on nuclear matters to persist is not satisfactory. We have 40% of the worlds yellow cake. We should channel Marie Antoinette and 'let them eat cake'. Josephine would agree.

Maybe now we are to have nuclear subs, we can open up the nuclear industry. We need to help people to understand the possibilities and see that nuclear is safer than driving a car. Would low-cost electricity make Olympic Dam instantly economic?

Bingle Bangle

Are you listening Scomo? Do you remember 'where the bloody hell are you'? Forget consensus and try some leadership. Jelly spine is not a good look. Maybe we should make Lara PM.

Electricity For The World

The Switkowski report is timorous. Where is the robust, purposeful advocacy for the bright future which can be enabled by nuclear power? Cheap power would enable the growth of the aluminium industry, mining, transport, the steel industry, agriculture, water management, construction, medicine, the cloud, defence, security, transport, home and office heating and cooling and much more.

Therefore it would pay for better hospitals and medical care, a salary for mothers, proper induction of our young, care of the elderly, funding for start-up businesses and sufficient military spending to deter potential invaders.

The 'electricity for the world' idea could feed Australians for 1,000 years, why are the people who understand this issue hiding in the long grass and keeping silent?

Recommendation; That we get on with the development of a nuclear industry in Australia. Prepare tender for nuclear reactors at Portland, Olympic Dam, Weipa, Pilbara, Darwin, Alice Springs, Jervis Bay and many more.

Recommendation: that an education program for Australians be developed to show that nuclear is a good idea and that it will pay for hospitals, schools, social welfare, productive industries and more.

Recommendation: that long-term electricity supply agreements be negotiated with the aluminium industry, the steel industry, mining industry, manufacturing and any other industries that need reliable low-cost power.

Recommendation: that courses in nuclear technology, power generation, network management, international negotiation, and other relevant disciplines be created and the students subsidised with both tuition and accommodation fees.

Perhaps we need new institutions for this. The current ones have failed.

SPACE

We Have Ignition

We have a nascent space industry. How do we help it grow?
Our ambition extends beyond being just a service provider because we have a dish on the other side of the world, to triangulate the position of satellites and moon shots.
We should be designing, building and launching satellites. Maybe we could specialise in mining applications or choose some industries, agriculture, fisheries, weather, security where space assets add value and lead the world.

Clarity

We need a proposal with the clarity of the Hydrogen Pitch. Instead the SIAA appears to have been captured by bureaucrats who aspire to work for the UN. We should liberate them to pursue this ambition.
SIAA report proclaims that the government should give the space industry money for vanity projects, to develop launch capabilities for use by others and to provide job opportunities for government bureaucrats.
SIAA 'Much of Australia's critical infrastructure relies on space-based assets'. What infrastructure? Vague pronouncements not adequate. Explain yourself make a case. Vague assertions are a waste of time. Sounds like a time serving bureaucrat.

Less Begging, More Action

We need less begging to the Australian Research Council and more definition of projects that deserve funding. What is the 'importance of space to all areas of government' another vague assertion needing connection to reality and benefit. Insight into operational drivers? What are they. Get past the waffle to specifics. If you do not know what they are, get out of the way and we will find someone who does. This statement amounts to we do not know what we are doing. Too much waffle in the style of Westminster. It is un-Australian and a waste of everyone's time.

What about security. Defence should fund both projects and research of value to Australia.

Sustainabollocks

Relevance to many international forums and multilateral issues - please detail these. UN goals on anything are irrelevant - especially something as vague and virtue signalling as sustainability. Are we trying to change the world by keeping it the same?

The UN is obsolete and ideologically corrupted. Sack these wafflers and get some serious people on board.

Forget space diplomacy and build some capability. We have too many bureaucratic jollies already. International agencies captured by lefties like you and therefore of less than zero value. This is bureaucratic bullshit of which Sir Humphrey would be proud.

Macbeth

Shakespeare in Macbeth captures the essence: 'It is a tale told by an idiot, full of sound and fury, signifying nothing'. Sack these clowns so that they can go to the UN and wallow in the indefinable 'sustainability'. We do not need cringing, waffling, gutless nobodies. The UN is full of them and would happily employ a few more, no outputs or results required.

Do Some Projects

We need to find someone who can identify, commission and direct projects like ARPA. Playing footsie with the ideological dreamers and morons at the UN is not satisfactory.

Recommendation: that we define how the space industry can support agriculture, water management, communications, security, perhaps swarm offensive capability, monitoring of shipping, flights, incoming missile detection, rail system management and initiate the projects.

Recommendation: that the federal government allocate the land and resources required for the launch facilities.

Recommendation: that new institutions be established to support, space, nuclear, aluminium and other priorities.

HYDROGEN

Repeat 'Net Zero By 2050' ... Again

Dr Alan Finkel has chaired a Hydrogen Working Group, tasked with developing a National Hydrogen Strategy. The report is very impressive, exploring technologies and possibilities. However their real goal is to liberate billions of dollars in government funding for the insiders and there is much talk of 'net zero by 2050'.

Dimsters

The utility of the phrase is that it is simple enough for dimsters, politicians, journalists, teachers and schoolchildren to learn and recite. Should we ask Dr. Finkel to explain why the zealots chant of' net zero by 2050' is the Holy Grail? Has he reviewed the unprofessional, inacurate and ideologically biased modelling behind this mantra? Does he really imagine that we can predict what will be happening in 2050? Would a serious scientist examine these predictions for validity?

Ministry Of Truth

We have been extensively and intensively brain-washed to think that these arbitrarily chosen numbers have some cosmic significance. They do. Cosmic rather than useful that is. The media is full of: 'net zero by 2050', 'net zero by 2050', 'net zero by 2050', 'net zero by 2050', 'net zero by 2050', 'net zero by 2050', especially the zealot zone at the ABC.

Does repetition make it more scientific Alan? Is it important because it is so often repeated? Has Alan abandoned science to enter politics or the dark arts of persuasion?

May I suggest some wider reading on the validity of climate modelling, they are not sound, depend upon arbitrary assumptions, ignore key causative factors, and are systematically mis-reported.

Also, please check out the contribution bushfires make to constituents of the atmosphere.

Lomberg, Plimer

Do these media morons know anything about climate or economic impacts? Not much. Have they read material by Bjorn Lomberg and Ian Plimer? I think not, they are on some ignorant Marxist cancel capitalism jihad. We seem to be eager to find triggers for hysteria. More brainstem brushing. It is not helpful. Hot news 23 October 2021 Twiggy has scored 3 Billion dollars from the NSW government to explore hydrogen based energy. Their submission was a masterpiece of political lobbying, congratulations. More votes from the climate religion children.

Lights Out

Do the mis-reporters understand the scam whereby electricity distributors must buy from the cheapest source at the moment of purchase, so when the sun is shining and the wind is blowing they must buy renewables. The base load generators are still running and generating costs for the supplier. So when the wind blows we are paying twice: for the base load generator and the windy stuff.

Bloviating in the wind. Apologies Bob, however you were a bit of a plagiarist, remember the Africa tour to steal some ideas.

Third World Reliability

Do these renewable sources provide reliable, continuous energy? If they had to provide reliable electricity, what would be the cost? Add the cost of pumped hydro and/or 'fill in' (dispatchable) gas plants and the renewable cost goes way up.

It is a cynical scam. Yet the morons in the media promote it as wonderful.

Smelter Frozen Full Of Congealed Aluminium

They excuse recent failures of the renewable strategy, lights out in South Australia, the Portland Aluminium Smelter frozen full of congealed aluminium. The government paid a high price (1 billion dollars) to restore the smelter to working order and support its future. Is this cost added to the price of renewables? I think not.

Simple answer is to put a nuclear power generating plant next to the smelter and we could have a leading role in the aluminium industry.

We now have the funding to explore hydrogen. Let us hope that it turns out to be useful.

AGRICULTURE

Water, Water, Everywhere

This industry is important, apart from feeding Australia, we already export $52 billion of fish, farm and forestry products, plus $12 billion of plant based products. Does everyone know this? Why not? Another failure of both the media and the schooling system.

What are the opportunities for further development? We have been talking for more than 100 years about harnessing Queensland and Arnhem Land rivers, turning them inland to create a food bowl.

Vast volumes of water pour into the ocean in many years. We need this water. It is time for action. If a couple of tree frogs have to relocate, no problem.

Damn It

If we built 5 dams per year, it would take 20 years. All the more reason to get started. We should also build here in Australia the turbines, pipes, trucks, irrigation systems, telemetry and software.

The government needs to kickstart this process. A long-term plan so that pipe manufacturers, truck manufacturers and all of the others can build the factories, organise their supply chains, hire, train the people and deliver the result at a reasonable price. Irresponsible and ignorant governments often have arbitrary and capricious purchasing patterns which do not allow the build up of the needed capabilities. More unproductive and foolish, short-term decisions by public servants, who are too lazy to find out how industry functions, that damage the life opportunities and the wellbeing of Australians. We pay their salaries and they betray us.

CSL was granted a monopoly in Australia and used this to launch business across the world.

Eyes on the prize, this idea could fund Australian prosperity and feed the locals for hundreds of years.

Snowy Grand Plan

We already have an international consulting business in the development of hydro-electric power, using the skills garnered in the development of the Snowy hydro-electric scheme. This could be expanded.

Get ready, we will soon be asking for a grand plan to manage the water resources of Australia. How come we have not bothered to make this plan already. Sound water management will make a massive difference to the life of Aussies and many industries.

So what have our politicians been doing? Asleep at the stick as usual, waxing on about some trivial bullshit worshipped in Mologlo Land.

Premium Preserved Food

Perhaps a specialisation in preserved food. There will be another pandemic, freight costs will rise, there may be a war, we should establish a position at the premium end of the preserved food chain. Maybe also ration packs for the military, not just ours. We know how to make a curry.

Delete government regulation and establish world-class inspection and certification procedures. Please note that the inspection does not create the quality. It is the farmers that create and deliver the fine produce.

Finest Food In The World

Brand Australia, the finest food in the world. We should ask 'Scotty from Marketing' to find Lara or Brittany and create a 'top table dining' campaign. By the way I detest the 'down under' description of Australia, it seems to have something to do with the romantic experiences of the US military in Sydney during World War Two. These are both insulting words.

'Top Table' could become our identity, both in the production and delivery of food, aluminium issues, Nuclear Issues and in geopolitical discussion.

The tired old European institutions have failed. We should enable the next phase of world development.

Turn Around Scotty

Scotty, listen up, what about 'dream time dining', 'walkabout dining', 'top drawer dining'. We can and should be on top. I still like 'Top Table'.

Forget the focus groups for a moment. As Steve Jobs said customer surveys are irrelevant because the punters do not know what is possible. They are looking out the back window and your job is to look forward. Are you listening Scotty? Turn around and look out the front window. If you had looked forward and seen what a disaster Malcolm would be, you might have allowed Tony Abbot to serve out the term he earned.

What have you done to earn your place? Cancelled 18c? Called out the climate bullshit and voted for a prosperous Australia? Jenny and the girls are counting on you to make things better. Appeasement and slithering are not a good look.

Call Australia For Action

How about an umbrella campaign with the theme 'call Australia for action'. Oh, maybe not. This might bring the America sailors back. Communication is such a bitch.

My personal preference is that we be known for doing stuff, not just nice beaches. Tourism is 'third world cringing', we need to 'stand up'.

Australia for a 'Top Table' experience.

Maybe Scotty is not the man for this job either.

In a pandemic riddled or is it addled world having fewer international visitors may be preferable.

Spectacular Events

Trade resources in every country to promote our food, aluminium, electricity, rails, bogies and more. Not an army of bureaucrats talking to one another, but spectacular events to put us on the map.

We need some substantial ambassadors, Gina, Twiggy, 'Titanic' Clive, Dame Nellie, The Don, Walter, Ita, Rupert, Russel, Mel, Kylie, Carl, Peta, Warnie, you choose. Flick the featherweights. I know some of these champions are no longer with us physically, however we may have a lingering reputation for providing the best in the world performance at opera, cricket and billiards.

We are on our way back to the top.

Recommendation: Create agriculture focussed institutions and whatever else is required, land allocation, streamlined regulation.

Recommendation: Commission research projects to focus on: production issues, funding issues, water issues, quality issues, preserving and packaging issues, exporting and logistics issues. Then do stuff.

Recommendation: Convene a summit so the industry participants can instruct government on what is required to enable the growth of these industries. Notice that the industry instructs the government, not government misappropriation of land and endless brainless regulations as happens now.

Recommendation: Design each of these processes so that the useful productive people flourish.

Banishment

Profiteering middle-persons should be banished. This is the land of opportunity for people who want to 'have a go', not for sly parasites.

BOOGIE WITH BOGIES

We Can Do It All

Imagine that anyone anywhere in the world who needed rails and bogies could call Australia and get design, manufacture, installation and operation and monitoring advice, systems and equipment. This would include track, sleepers, shingle, points, control systems, signals, driver training software, track condition monitoring and perhaps automated trains. Traffic management systems, perhaps via satellites.
Buffet thinks that rail will be back. We should enable the wave.

Export Train Driver Training Systems

Did you know that we have been exporting 'train driver training' software to India since the 1980s?
Less shipping of low value iron ore around the world, instead we should do rails, I beams, mesh etc. Maybe we could get into high speed trains. We certainly have the need to cover large distances in a cost effective manner.

Bogies, Wheels, Rails

Then, let us select some other downstream manufacture targets and be the world champion. What if we supplied the bogies, wheels and rails and the locals built their own carriages? That was the profile of the car companies in the 1920s. Designed to be knocked down and shipped. Boogie with bogies.
If we converted less that 20% of our iron ore production into

steel we would earn an additional $65 billion dollars and add 50,000 jobs.

There are many, many opportunities.

Robotic, Additive, Manufacturing

We need a modern manufacturing strategy. In a robotic world, labour cost is insignificant. Short run manufacturing can be economic. Additive manufacturing provides flexibility. We can do the product design, the production design, build and supply the machines and the materials. These can be exported. Alternatively we could do the manufacturing here. Depends upon shipping costs, skills and resources in the client country and our diplomacy.

Better still we could make the design software that fed off to robotic construction or additive manufacturing.

Designing and building the robots and the additive manufacturing machines would be a step in the right direction. We need managers with vision, bankers with a long-term view and a government that cares about the future.

Mittelstand

Germany has many 'mittelstand', middle sized companies that supply specialised machinery, for example the ashphalt cooking, road making machines we see here. There must be industries where Aussies can be the gurus and design and build the specialised machinery.

We know that Italian tiles are special. George Limb advised me that tile-making machines, made in Germany and operated in Brazil provide low-cost, high quality tiles. Changes the industry.

Less Sizzle, More Steak

Our cosseted government officials who need a prosperous Australia to pay both their salaries and their superannuation, might learn to buy Australian. We do not need hand-holding and undergraduate pronouncements about supply chains, or blather like this 'For Australia to be recognised as a high-quality and sustainable manufacturing nation that helps to deliver a strong, modern and resilient economy for all Australians.' More of this bureaucrat-pleasing sustainability nonsense. We do not seek recognition we seek trade. Enough sizzle, give me some steak.

We rode on the sheep's back because Britain was fighting wars and needed our wool to make uniforms. We must again connect with the world and provide products and services that are in demand.

Get On With It

The opportunities are legion.
It is time to get moving.

WASTING WEALTH

Nuclear Family Explodes

Once upon a time, the most important institution was the family, not the experimental two people against the world 'nuclear' family, but the extended family with uncles, aunts and the extended diaspora. You may have noticed that the nuclear family has a tendency to explode, it is a failed experiment.

Solitaries

Recently the government has set out to replace the family, so that a one person household is a valid option. It really isn't, we are a social species and living alone is not good for your diet or your esprit. However if you live alone you may need government support, so they capture your vote. Is this cynical approach designed to destroy the family, to create dependence and capture the vote of the solitaries?
Advice to singles: 'If you hate being single, just go on a dating app. You'll enjoy being single so much more.'

Subjugation

It is about control, families tend to be self sufficient, the overlord wants dependence and tax revenue. Conscription, tax, religion, wheat and electricity have each been used to assert central power and downgrade the family. Stalin liked the control that comes from central supply of electricity.

Before that we had the 'breadwinner' who provided funds and security, worked well for some, others shriek 'patriarchy' and stamp their feet. Further back, we had the mother as the centre of the culture, with everyone else in a support role. Maybe we could bring this model back. Conduct a 'parliament of mothers' so that we can get some advice on how our society should operate.

First, let us have a look at some of our current institutions.

How Much Is Enough?

There are some institutions that deliver useful functions, we should welcome them and ensure that the intended result is delivered in an efficient and effective manner. Please register efficient and effective, doing the right things and performing them with modest resources.

Can there be too much schooling, doctoring, lawyering and government interference? Yes there can. These institutions have grown like topsy. Who decides the scope of services and who measures the efficiency and effectiveness?

In the following pages we argue that processes must be found to limit the wanton, self-interested expansion of institutions. Some schooling, doctoring, lawyering and government regulation is useful. How much is enough?

Quality

Are the services delivered by our institutions and the people working in them as good as they should be? We don't know. Most of us just deal with what exists, because it is not clear how quality control can be exercised.

Remember 'King Rat' by Clavell, set in a Japanese POW camp, someone will work out how to 'thread the needle' and flourish in every environment. Lobbyists twist policy to suit their paymasters, they are not working for us. Ideally government would 'keep the ring' and allow useful people to flourish.

Would more worthwhile and civilised people prosper if we had better institutions? Clearly. It is up to us to define and demand the improvements. Good guys should not finish last.

Too Extensive, Too Expensive And Of Variable Quality

Unfortunately government institutions are above the law and exercise brute force which restricts our freedom and distorts the conduct of society. We are the consumers of these services and we should be getting an appropriate range of services, a satisfactory quality of service at an appropriate price.

Currently they are too extensive, too expensive of variable quality and still expanding.

Who decides the range, quality and price of these services? Do we just let the members of each profession make range, quality and price decisions for themselves?

Odd Couple

The odd couple of Adam Smith and George Bernard Shaw alert us to the tendency for members of a profession to look after their own self-interest, 'conspiracy against the laity'. OK, perhaps we are accustomed to people taking decisions in their own self interest, we all do it every day. It works well for a banker, a bank robber, a shopper or a share trader. So, is this really a problem?

Well, yes it is. At one time Australia had the highest rate of hysterectomies in the world. Was this something weird about our women, or our surgeons? Australia has high rates of retention in schooling. Does this translate into superior economic performance and a caring community, or was it just a Keating scam to lower the unemployment numbers?

Wood tells us that "Experts don't know when to stop ... If they are charged with maintaining clean waterways, they'll exert authority over every puddle and seek to license beavers". Just so. These institutions touch everyone's life and we hope that the range, quality and price decisions relating to these services will be taken with regard to the 'community interest'.

If there is such a thing as the 'community interest'. Some average experience that should apply to everyone?

Freemium

Perhaps the average experience can be available for free or at a low price, while tailored experiences are available for higher fees? On the internet this is called 'freemium' many experiences for free, money made on the 10% who pay for refined services. We already have public and private schooling, public and private medicine and legal fees ranging from zero to astronomical, and there are many government handouts. Did anyone design these systems? Are they subject to the reality check of natural selection? We can do much better.

Trickle Down

Early expressions of schooling, doctoring, lawyering and license granting were targeted to benefit the rich because they could pay. We had Eton, the Royal Physicians, Magna Carta and the East India Company. In our democratic age the lower orders are offered some ill-considered 'trickle down to the masses', bureaucratic institutional echoes of the exclusive services enjoyed by the rich.

Ladder Of Equity

Julia wanted 40% of the populace to have a degree. Why not 100%? This was a variety of 'class envy'. We want what they have got. The middle class have a degree, so my job is to get a degree for the working class. Notice the narrow ideological frame of this decision making.

Victoria University thought of itself as the ladder of opportunity for 'Westies'. So, put people into TAFE for 2 years at low-cost, then transfer them to the University for a year and give them a degree. Job done. Equality of outcome.

I had students in my 3rd year class who had never had an abstract idea in their life and just wanted to know, 'what am I supposed to say'? More parrot than intellectual. Three years wasted for what? Is the student better off? Is the the society better off? Feels like 'window dressing'. Devalues the whole system don't you think?

So these institutions that the rest of us deal with, were they designed to support the mass of citizens in the conduct of their everyday life? No, they were not.

20 Years In Prison

It suits the rich - people for whom the worship of money is a high priority - to abandon their children into the schooling system for 20 years until they emerge as a doctor, a lawyer or politician. No time wasted talking to children, full focus on the next money-making scam.

The rest of us cannot afford to blow 20 years in a prison that prevents us from learning about the world, denies us the opportunity to earn and teaches very little of value. Some further thoughts on schooling in a later section.

The point is that services designed to suit the majority of people would not be the same as those created to indulge the whims of the prosperous, pleasured and pampered classes. It is time to re-imagine the design of our services and institutions to ensure that they are suited to the needs of everyday people.

Prevention Or Cure?

Should we focus on prevention or cure. Many of our current institutions have an 'ambulance chasing' mentality, where they seek praise for 'picking up the pieces' after the main event. Much of the operation of the Law and Medicine follows this principle. It is therefore in their interest to promote the problem they ostensibly cure to ensure the continuity of funding. The NHS in Britain spend 40% of their budget on preventible disease, not much on prevention.

Is it possible to shift the focus to prevention? Difficult for the institutions to even consider shrinking as their funding depends upon the persistence of the original problem. Counselling anyone?

Economists are supposed to understand incentives, maybe we should ask them. We need incentives that lead to problems being prevented, rather than perpetuated.

Bogus Institutions

Parroting drivel from UN, WHO, World Bank, OECD, WTO and all other corrupt and ideologically flawed institutions, is both irresponsible and pathetic. They are staffed by refugees who could not earn a legitimate living doing something useful. They do not need to sponsor a refugee program, they are a refugee program.

We should stop wasting money on these bogus institutions. Was the World Health Organisation useful during the Covid pandemic? No, they spread lies that distorted our response and covered for China. Time to spend our money on competent Aussies instead of international featherweights.

We should classify these obsolete international institutions as terrorist organisations and prohibit their entry to Australia. We would be much better off without their corrupt, self serving nonsense, brain-washing both our polity and our children.

Bombast From Brussels - Shut Up Ursula

Much of their blather is tired, lefty, communist-echo rubbish from Europe. Europe has had its strut. We need to move on. Following Europe as it declines into irrelevance makes no sense. Germany abandons nuclear energy at the moment when it is most needed. The EU opens the borders to all comers, destroying its identity. Bombast from Brussels, we do not need it. Shut up Ursula, you are just a mouthpiece for the swampsters. and have zero democratic legitimacy.

Europe set out to evangelise the world with stories most of its own people no longer believe. Turns out that the 'Dream time' stories from Australia have equal legitimacy and much greater longevity. The fantasy of European superiority is finished. Everyone has guns now.

Who Dares Wins

In our multicultural society, we should render this 'assertion' in some of the hundreds of languages available across the world eg. Latin: 'Qui audet adipiscitur', French: 'Qui ose gagne', German: 'Wer wagt, gewinnt', Polish: 'Kto ryzykuje, wygrywa', Russian: 'Победа храбрым достается', Chinese: '誰敢贏' … whatever. In French I prefer 'vouloir c'est pouvoir'.

Our current institutions are closer to the mirror-image expression, that 'pioneers get arrows'.

There was a time when the people who took the risk - from kings to hunters and mothers - got the benefit. Not anymore. Sly, selfish, ill-informed, cowardly and irresponsible decision makers - often government bureaucrats - are grabbing benefits for themselves and screwing up the world.

Taleb advises that those without 'skin in the game' take bad decisions, because they have no accountability and no adverse outcomes for themselves. Bankers who can crash the international finance system while paying themselves very fat bonuses and then be paid out with trillions of dollars of other people's money. These same bankers having been rewarded for their greed and stupidity are poised to crash the system again. Who dares wins indeed.

Financial Terrorism

It is Financial Terrorism. Remember the Fed in 2007, give us $700 million today or we will collapse the world financial system. The improper and inappropriate transfers to bankers later grew to trillions of dollars. Add them to the terrorist list. They have done more damage than 'ISIS'. The politicians who give them the money should also be on the list.
It is the productive people who pay the bill for this monstrous theft.

Aristophanes And Lysistrata

If the public poseurs are venal and incompetent, who do we turn to? Reach for a classic solution. Aristophanes (c. 440-380 bc), 'Athens's problems could be solved only by little people of no importance, not the greedy, vain and incompetent leaders in the public eye'.
Maybe we should reach for Lysistrata. Even then, there were some 'black legs' who kept the shop open.

Whirling Dervishes

Europe seemed important because they got the machine gun - invented in America - ahead of other people and slaughtered the opposition. Nothing admirable there. The British garnered a large empire, not because they had created a superior society - it is much more straightforward - they had the guns.
Churchill praised the courage of the whirling dervishes at the battle of Omdurman in Egypt in 1898 as they charged towards the British machine guns and tens of thousands of them were obliterated. It is time to reject European hubris.
Time for Nemesis.

Palaeolithic Emotions, Mediaeval Institutions

Harvard biologist Wilson observes that we humans have palaeolithic emotions, mediaeval institutions and god-like technologies. It is not clear that we are smart enough to understand the working of the current systems, and our record of designing new systems is abysmal. Fascism and Communism failed. Capitalism produces a very wide range of outcomes, from palatial to penurious.

Big Brain Design

The designers of Brasilia missed a few details, for example there was nowhere for the construction workers to live, so the process depended on an unplanned shanty town built next door. The designers of the West Gate Bridge modelled the structure to ensure that it could carry the loads required. Unfortunately, they did not model the stresses on the structure during construction, leading to a section falling and killing 37 people. More unfortunate again is that the same problem - with a similar design - had occurred with the Cleddau Bridge in Wales four months earlier.

It is the same with our social-engineering, some unintended consequences.

Doom And Collapse

Many temporarily glorious cultures and cities have disappeared. Pandemics may have led to the collapse of historical civilisations (see Doom by Niall Ferguson, Guns Germs and Steel and Collapse by Jared Diamond).

Niall Ferguson wrote a book about the decay of institutions, I recommend it 'It is our laws and institutions that are the problem'.

These systems for delivery of services are exceedingly complex and have long term consequences. They are difficult to understand, and designing something better is very difficult.

Modular

Ideally we would have a modular structure where the users choose the services that suit them best and inferior services disappear. Effective memes have been mimicked for millennia and still are. Having many villages or tribes each following their own individual understanding of best practice is a modular structure That is why this format has enabled our survival for millennia.

Robbing Hood

The dream that progressive income tax would have a 'Robin Hood' effect and take from the rich to give to the poor, turned into a nightmare. It did not work because the rich have an army of mercenaries in the legal and tax domains that help them to dodge paying their share of income tax and to get away with their money-making scams. The tax and law mercenaries are second order parasites who live much better than they deserve, their contribution to prosperity is less than zero. We will free them up to get a useful job.

This highlights the paradox that a significant proportion of government expenditure goes to protecting the property of the rich. They get great benefit, but do not pay their share. Many people including 'lady luck' helped them to 'score', we shall teach them to 'share'.

Lugubrious

We will not be exploring Jared Diamond's ecology focussed five factors in societal decline, however the 'grab baggy' item 5: 'a society's response to environmental, political, social and economic problems' suggests the need for sound design and the need for some knowledge beyond ornithology for the lugubrious Jared.

Gherkin, Empire State, Harbour Bridge

Perhaps the systems that worked best were the tribal and familial structures that have been the basis of our life for millions of years. At least they were sustainable, equitable, low carbon, diverse, socially distanced, without chatter about economics, gender, class or race and no power-crazed loon enslaving everyone in order to build a bigger pyramid, Gherkin, Empire State, Harbour Bridge, ship, plane, tank, railroad, perhaps even pretending to hold back the tide, promising to 'eliminate' Covid 19 or promoting gender dysphoria to primary school children.

Stone Age Skills

What we forget is that these traditional approaches were not static structures, at some times of the year small groups moved about and fed themselves, at other times large, sometimes very large groups gathered for festivals or ceremonies. Social structure adapted to season, occasion and resource availability. Small groups in winter when diseases spread, large celebrations in summer when they do not. Seems obvious, non? How come our modern apparatchiks do not understand this basic idea?

No Hair Dryers Or Sandals

Do we want to turn the clock back? We may not have a choice. Following a meteor strike, major pandemic, nuclear holocaust or Extinction Rebellion victory, fancy technologies will not longer be available and stone-age skills will rule. Is this what the apocalypse apologists want? Did anyone tell them that there will be no electricity, supermarkets, sandals, hair dryers, beard trimmers or Instagram?

Psychopath On Top

However, if we were seeking to design a world where modern technologies were available without the megalomaniacs, and with professions and institutions that delivered appropriate services, would there be a precedent? Yes there is, Graeber and Wengrow in 'The Dawn of Everything' describe ancient societies that lived in harmony without the psychopath on top. Acemoglu and Robinson suggest the need for a balance between greedy elites and concerned citizens.

Could we reach for this ideal? What would it look like?

Well, democracy was supposed to limit the power of both the narcissists and the government. The political structures needed to implement a governance design are available. What about taking the design decisions?

Infantilising Nanny State

The authors of the Australian Constitution imagined a world where Aussies could create their own life experience, embrace initiative, innovation and independence, achieving for themselves, liberation, prosperity, security and delight. We need to revisit these aspirations, get the government hand out of our pocket and the amoral, obsessive and intrusive regulators off our backs.

The tyranny of the infantilising nanny state turns us all into beggars. They assert the right to control too many aspects of our life, limiting creativity, opportunity, living space and prosperity.

Enough Already

How much government is enough? What should the role of government be? What schooling should be available? Should it be compulsory? Who builds and staffs the hospitals? What rules do we need and how might they be administered?

The Australian constitution was a good start. However, since then our institutions and professions have greatly expanded their reach. Was this expansion designed? Is it in the best interests of the citizens? Who benefits and who pays?

The record shows that the productive people have been punished at the behest of and for the benefit of the passengers.

Flick The Failures

Perhaps it is time to review our progress, to think through how our professions and institutions should be serving the interests of Aussies, to consider how recent technologies might be applied and to reset our course.

First we need to design systems that work for the mass of citizens. Then we might ask, what is the feedback process that enables the continuous improvement of these systems and services? Currently, the insiders just grab more and more to pleasure themselves?

Popper recommends that we flick the failures in the political class.

Politicians in a democracy should govern with consent, not consensus. Politicians like consensus because no one is responsible. Democracy functions more effectively when specific people are responsible for specific policies so that we can vote them out if we do not like the outcome, correcting the error of their election.

Requisite Variety

Do we have the requisite variety specified by Wallace and Darwin? A range of services so that natural selection can operate and we can eliminate the unfit and keep the best. To some extent, however many institutions are monolithic and rigid, continuing long after their value has diminished.

The delivery frameworks for schooling, doctoring, lawyering and regulating are rigid, static and narrow, the product of human brain limited design, not the naturally selected, sophisticated fruit of evolution. This is why indigenous cultures in Australia and America where everyone got something to eat and had somewhere to sleep were more sophisticated than the callous European misadventure where people could starve, be homeless, die or be exiled to the other side of the world..

Perhaps the enlightenment experiment was triggered by insights from tribal life in America.

Adaptation

We seek an adaptive design where new ideas can be tried and expanded if they deliver value. These issues are exceedingly complex and deserve careful and detailed consideration. If we could envision a framework to allow such examination, a series of task forces with engineers, scientists, statisticians, model builders with an occasional lawyer or medico. The mission would be to design structures that allow evolution, not some static prescription - as we do now - that would soon be obsolete and ineffective.

We now think that our early societies were complex, experimental and forever adaptive, some seasons more hunting other seasons more planting, with great variety across the world.

It is time we allowed some adaptive structures in our institutions so that we can favour the fruitful and winnow the woke.

Yappers

Yappers from the fluffy fringe, not welcome. Narcissistic virtue signalling has less than zero value and should be ignored. Morons in the media with limited cognitive capacity, love to recite these fashionable clichés, as discussing the complexity of life is beyond them. The complexity and uncertainty central to modelling life decades into the future are reduced to 'net zero by 2050'. This infantile idea, with Orwellian levels of repetition creates a cult and the opportunity to persecute unbelievers. Do we remember the Spanish Inquisition?

Government funded mono-cultural, biased broadcasters violate their charters, by employing, encouraging and promoting these illegitimate yappers. The Greens are in parliament because of extensive, free and improper party political airtime. These broadcasters are a cancer on society and must be excised. Simple as ABC.

Mind Your Own Business

They also have no right to meddle in your private affairs. If you wish to make some lamingtons for the fete as your mother and grandmother did, go ahead. No need for government inspectors to invade your kitchen and make some imperial pronouncements. If you wish to build something for sale or provide a paid service to others, it is none of their business, go ahead.

Your child should not have to pay tax on the revenue made by mowing the neighbour's lawn, take out insurance, or get an occupational health and safety permit. Tell them to 'bugger off' and mind their own business.

Rise Twice

We are not seeking to specify perfect recipes. There are no perfect recipes … except in the kitchen, and even then … Soufflé anyone? Will Andrew be back? Was Keating channelling some power over the afterlife?

Good Ideas Flourish

What we are looking for is a framework that allows the forces of evolution to operate, where bad ideas fail and good ideas spread. A marketplace of ideas as operates in tribal cultures, rather than the coercive power exercised from the centre by the megalomaniac or more recently by ignorant, narcissistic government apparatchiks.

Let us step back a little, have a look at some of our institutions and consider our choices.

SCHOOLING

Ivan The Terribly Thoughtful

Ivan Illich, who wrote 'De-Schooling Society' delivered a brilliant exposition in Wilson Hall at Melbourne University in 1972. I was there. We experienced some revelations, for example, on the impact of compulsory schooling and institutional subservience:

'... we have come to realise that for most people the right to learn is curtailed by the obligation to attend school ...

The pupils are thereby "schooled":

- to confuse teaching with learning,

- grade advancement with education,

- a diploma with competence, and

- fluency with the ability to say something new.

Their imagination is "schooled" to accept service in place of value.

Medical treatment is mistaken for health care, social work for the improvement of community life, police protection for safety, military poise for national security, the rat race for productive work. Health, learning, dignity, independence, and creative endeavour are defined as little more than the performance of the institutions which claim to serve these ends, and their improvement is made to depend on allocating more resources to the management of hospitals, schools, and other agencies in question.'

Pat Vort-Ronald identifies the brainwashing, 'ideological hegemony' to produce docile snowflakes and 'commodity fetishism' to replace learning stuff with buying stuff.

We have had access to these ideas for almost 50 years, have we understood them and considered how to improve our life experience? Apparently not.

Chat Match

Illich suggested that it might be beneficial if people with similar interests could get together and chat. Inspired by this I sought to implement this idea and tried to place an ad for 'Chat Match'. The Herald refused to run the ad.

Not one to take 'no' for an answer I escalated my enquiry and ended up speaking with an editor. He was utterly confident of his right to arbitrarily censor advertisements in the paper. Perhaps if I had been the source of significant advertising revenue it would have been different. His declaration 'you might be creating a cult like 'Scientology' and therefore your ad will not appear'.

Fifty years later we have Facebook, Instagram, Tik Toc, What's App and more each creating their own echo-chamber. Ivan would have hoped that the conversation would be more interesting.

Delete Universities, Create New Institutions

Niall Ferguson has decided that the way forward is to start a new university 'However, having taught at several, including Cambridge, Oxford, New York University and Harvard, I have also come to doubt that the existing universities can be swiftly cured of their current pathologies.'

It is time for us to start new institutions, Melbourne has become moron-ville, as an alumnus, I am embarrassed by the ill-informed, ideological drivel oozing out under the portals.

Wilde, Churchill, Marx

We should more deeply explore the difference between education and schooling, was it Wilde who said, 'nothing that is worth knowing can be taught … the real schools should be the streets' and Churchill with, 'my education was only interrupted by my schooling'. Marx in 1866 proposed that every child from the age of 9 should be engaged in productive labour, we should all have the opportunity to learn and should 'work in order to be able to eat'.

In contemporary western societies young people spend 20 years in a fantasy asylum without work, controlled and conditioned by people who have negligible experience of actual productive work or life. The teachers went from school to university and then back to school. A snowflake production process.

School teachers who imagine that they are entitled to a greater say than parents about what should happen to the children are simply being impertinent.

Watch, Learn, Do

Our long term survival as a species has depended upon the fact that our brains are very good at, even optimised for, 'observational learning' - watch, learn, do. In a traditional tribal environment 'observational learning' happens all day every day. In the artificial, stunted, ritualised school environment, small-minded teachers dominate, children obey and both stay ignorant about how things happen in the outside world. One of the functions of school is to force children to understand that they must grovel before the power of the state.

No wonder these children emerge as frightened little snowflakes, begging for a government cloak to 'keep them safe'. Programmed to support #Istandwithdan, clearly this indoctrination is very effective. Hysteria and fear.

How did it come to this?

Aping Our Betters

We were all locked up in school for 20 years and therefore think that experience, or is it the absence of experience, is normal. Are we just 'aping our betters'? That the English ruling class sent their children to weird asylums from the age of 8, does not mean that this was good for these 'privileged' children or that everyone should have a similar experience.

The 'adult' members of the aristocracy - where beauty meets money - were busy drinking champagne, going to parties and balls, buying their sons an officer role, their daughters a suitable husband or perhaps ensuring the continuity of their privilege through parliament.

Babies were hand-passed off to a wet-nurse, producing an unfortunate consequence where the next pregnancy arrived promptly, women had large numbers of children and died early. Children were a nuisance and therefore were sent to a remote prison for a long sentence. This may help to explain the dysfunctional psychopathology among so many of the aristocracy.

Is our current focus on the misnamed 'child care', where children are abandoned by their mothers into the control of a low paid substitute, an echo of this aristocratic expediency?

Are We All Aristocrats?

Eton, Harrow, Charterhouse and Radley are no more than expensive, class ridden, child-minding schemes, seeking to keep the network closed, entrench the power of the ruling clique and are not a suitable model for mass schooling. Richard Beard in 'Sad Little Men' suggests that the self-important and emotionally stunted people produced by these institutions, like Boris and Dave should not be in positions of authority.

Boris still imagines that it is his job to meddle in the lives of 'Bloody Northeners', rather than to get out of the way and let them look after themselves. Note to Petronella, Carrie or any of the others: 'please get Boris to watch "Peaky Blinders"'.

Clinton backed availability over style, expediency rules. Beware

of 'buyers remorse'.
No cigar.

Grooming

As we sought to grasp the meaning of democracy, we imagined that giving every child an experience modelled on the aristocracy would be appropriate.
Forcing all children to participate in some pale 'echo of Eton' is absurd. What were we thinking? Does it make sense to groom every child to be a Prime Minister in 18th Century England? How could we be so stupid?

Lobotomy

We should have another look at the choices available for the induction of our young in the modern world. There are more interesting and more useful activities beyond the extensive time-wasting, narrowness, shallowness and conformity of the school system. Many of our teachers are pathetic, ignorant little nobodies lobotomising our children, killing enthusiasm, creativity and individuality?

Sit Still

Much of the knowledge of the world is available on the internet, therefore forcing children to 'sit still' in rows in a classroom listening to some ignorant, fugitive is not necessary and not appropriate. Children start out energetic, enthusiastic, searching and adventuring. By the end of their schooling, they are crippled, cringing castrati. Try to overcome the brain-washing you have received about the value of schooling and liberate both yourself and your children from this stultifying experience.

Just Do It

Tradies used to leave school at 14 and get on with the job. What was wrong with that? Nurses used to leave home at 16 and learn on the job. What was wrong with that? Farmers were learning farm skills from a very young age and should not be forced to waste years listening to some irrelevant curriculum. Soldiers have been recruited in their early teens for millennia.

Ballerinas and tennis players can attend school half-time and spend the rest of the day building their skills. What is wrong with that? Should this opportunity be made available to all students?

Much of schooling is like the peacocks tail ... an unnecessary affectation. How much of the stuff you were forced to recite at school has helped you to live your life?

Barista, Barrister, Beautician, Bureaucrat Or Bludger

For many decades, school was where you learnt that you were not smart enough to be a brain surgeon or a barrister and that you should be grateful for the opportunity to be a barista, beautician or a bumbling bureaucrat.

In contrast, our contemporary snowflakes are taught at school that they are entitled to high self-esteem and respect, before they have either knowledge or achievement and that you can be a brain surgeon, barrister, blogger or bludger, as you wish.

Perhaps you may concede that it is time to let the scales fall from our eyes and explore these issues.

Begetting, Gestating, Birthing

Parents play the principal role in the begetting, gestating, birthing and then the extensive and expensive preparation of their children for life. Parental rights are more important than the assertions of any of the interfering busybodies. What are the elements of this preparation: feeding, toilet training, speech, counting, putting clothes on, civilised behaviour towards others, play, making the bed, keeping room tidy, spelling, writing, arithmetic, geography, history and whatever else the parent wishes to put on the list. For example find your special skill, develop your talents, contribute to the world.

Mozart, Early 10,000 Hours

What do they say is required to launch a career as a ballerina … an ambitious mum. Having a parent or partner who cares can enable success at tennis (Agassi, Docic), chess (Polgár), cooking (Child), music (Mozart), politics (Bush) and gardening (Klein), whatever suits the skill set and interests of the child. The parent is better placed to make these decisions than any outsider. Early commitment is part of the recipe for success, get those 10,000 hours done. Mozart was touring Europe playing in public concerts at the age of six.

The child should be allowed to develop these skills, rather than being locked up at a remote location, forced to listen to ignorant clowns who imagine that they have the right to exercise fascist control, while brainwashing their charges with their own personal fetishes - primary student gender dysphoria or worship of the Climate Gods.

Find Your Calling

The politicians, teachers and bureaucrats are not smarter or more ethical than the parents, despite the proclamations of Terry McAuliffe. They have much less knowledge of the potential of the child and much less 'skin in the game' than the parents. Decision making on schooling has been abandoned to the wrong people. It is a command for submission by who? Is there someone who has the right to imprison and brainwash your children for 20 years? I think not. We must force these jerk-offs back into their own dark, moist corner. Parents rule.

These apparatchiks simply wish to perpetuate the scams that enable their undeserved standard of living.

In Sweden children do not go to school until the age of 10. The early life experience should be tailored to the needs of the specific child. Parents have the insight and level of care required to pursue this goal. Outsiders do not.

Open Your Eyes

Our current system values teacher tyranny and narrow subservience over observational learning. We should encourage our young to get out more, visit a farm, bank, factory, mine and/or go fruit picking, build a house, establish a garden, pull down the engine of a car to see how it works, start a company, play nurses and doctors, do something. I was wandering around a butter factory, riding in the delivery truck, swimming in the creek and going duck shooting in Tangambalanga at the age of ten.

Traditional cultures would mobilise the young to get in the harvest. We should do the same. Send these adolescents to do something useful, starting the fruit picking in Queensland and coming south with the sun. Training tome, Ray Lawler's 'Summer of the Seventeenth Doll'.

Mediocrity

Many teachers are fugitives. Most of them stumbled through school, did not have the courage to take on a role where they would have to perform (make or sell something), a couple of years in an easy-entry, low-grade course and back into school. How can poor performance at school be a qualification to become a teacher?

Our schools are populated by whingers and parasites, so it is not surprising that the students become infected with a bleak view of the world and lack the capacity to build a life. Meanwhile the teachers congratulate themselves and demand gratitude and applause from both students and parents. The gratitude should flow the other way.

Why do we tolerate their mediocrity?

Grovel

No responsible parent would force their children to grovel before this garbage. Some diminutive harridan forced my son to sit on the floor to nourish her feelings of importance. There was no problem, she just wanted to demonstrate her power. He was not in her class, simply passed her in the corridor. No child should ever be forced to the floor. Perhaps she should join Victoria Police, get a baton, pepper spray and some rubber bullets.

I spent half an hour speaking with the deputy principal about the incident. She imagined that she had the right to tell me what words I could use and in her imperial capacity dismissed the incident. No shortage of attitude, after all I was an irrelevant parent.

Where is the life experience here? What do they know about the world? Not much. Why do we allow these uneducated, inexperienced people to direct and dominate our children for 20 years. It is self-harm.

No wonder our children are ignorant, pathetic, whingeing snowflakes. Worse still they graduate with an unfounded sense of self-importance, asserted by teachers and not based on knowing or doing anything. 'Everyone gets a prize'. This is popular with teachers because they are not themselves good enough to win prizes in competitive environments.

Apocalypse

We should stop teachers from terrorising students with ill-informed, apocalyptic nonsense about issues neither party understands. Why do people listen to school truant and 'teenage savant' Greta. You will of course have asked yourself if 'teenage savant' is an oxymoron.

In Pauline Hanson's latest revelation, Adam Bandt sails off with Greta into the sunset in a tiny Titanic. Bon voyage.

Parents Trump Bureaucrats

It is time to show some respect for parents and allow our children to learn and grow. The parents have the right to, and should, choose what happens to their kids. How did we ever imagine that imperious, ignorant bureaucrats would do a better job than parents?

To allow some evolution, schooling should no longer be compulsory.

Recommendation 1: Schooling should become voluntary. Let the parents decide. Ballerinas, boxers, painters, musicians, sculptors, divas, sports people will all do better with less time wasted in school.

Follow your dream and enrich the world.

WELLBEING

Or Is It Health, Perhaps Life?

Nutrition, exercise, meditation ... caring for the body and the mind - if they can be separated - followed by the treatments for cuts, bruises, disease and disenchantment. Should we focus on prevention or cure? In the NHS in the UK spending on treatment of preventable diseases takes 40% of the funding while very little is spent on prevention.

How come we have an epidemic of lassitude, obesity and gloom? Clearly prevention is not working too well. What about cure? That is working better. Why is that? People get paid to perform the remediation.

Perhaps we should diminish the extent of coercion, less force, more freedom, so that people can find a meaningful life for themselves and be both healthier and happier.

Paradoxically, we refer to the treatment of medical problems as the 'health' system. An interesting choice of words. Perhaps it is the aspiration for a return to 'health'. Surely 'health' should apply to the entire cycle including prevention, discovery and remediation, perhaps to all of life.

Follow Your Dream

What about allowing the citizens to find their own meaningful mission in life. Would that have an effect upon wellbeing? I think so. Did Zuckerberg enjoy starting Facebook, Jobs - Apple, Gates - Microsoft, Hewlett and Packard - HP, Musk - Tesla, Knight - Nike, Branson - Brides, Rupert - News and so on? Of course they did. All of them are a bit twitchy, so they could have ended badly. Zuckerberg had some help from the Winklevoss twins, the Apple 1 computer was built by Steve Wozniak while working full time at HP, Gates learnt the trade from Paul Allen, Bill and Dave were encouraged by Terman from Stanford, Elon learnt that bankers were rich and dumb while at the Bank of Nova Scotia, Knight just wanted to overcome the embarrassment from always being second in college foot races, Branson was always full of bravado, Rupert had ink in his veins and a fine parental example.

If we could lower the barriers, more people could establish a business, provide a product or service that other people value, without having to grovel to the government for permission, spend ridiculous amount of time getting approval, tolerate unreasonable, imperial intrusion by the regulators and pay the army of expensive advisers.

Allowing the parasite class in their regulatory role to obstruct and punish the productive people is not appropriate and leads to bad outcomes.

Creating Criminals

Perhaps people turn to crime, because starting and running a legitimate business entails too much grovelling to regulators. We should be allowed some self-respect, non? Please consider that again, if you do not enjoy being abused by arrogant, illegitimate regulators, crime, drugs or depression are available options. Alternatively, we could minimise the regulation and allow people to have a life. Hear me, regulation creates crime, obesity and drug use.

Imagine that most of the people, most of the time were engaging in activities that they found meaningful and rewarding. Would that improve our health? I think so. It would also diminish the incidence of theft, drugs and depression.

Current rules prohibit people from making cheese at home. We have been making cheese at home for how long? Certainly hundreds of years. How can we allow some brainless, regulatory goon to block this normal behaviour?

Notice that allowing people to have a life is the answer, not more government rules, regulations and ruckus, or is it rictus.

'Health' Decisions

Many citizens are pleased with the service they receive from the health system in Australia. Many practitioners do a fine job. Nurses on call provide a most valuable service.

However, there are a very large number of bureaucrats smothering the health service, demanding extensive, expensive and badly designed reporting and compliance and forcing unsound decision-making onto the profession, to suit the bureaucrat rather than the doctor or the patient. These interlopers are a waste of money. What about getting a job where you add some value?

One study showed that surgeons spend only 10% of their time holding the knife. Surely we can design the process better to allow them to get on with their real job?

Dodging the lawyers and regulators plus paying excessive insurance fees creates unsound recommendations from doctors. Allowing decisions in the best interests of the patient would be preferable.

Big Picture

We have an opportunity to redesign the system to more quickly and efficiently connect patients with the training, advice and treatment they need. This design should be conducted by a team including physicists, scientists, engineers, mathematicians, actuaries, economists, nurses and doctors.

The brief should be to redesign the system from the ground up. No tinkering at the edges. Please notice that we respect the medical profession's expertise in diagnosis and delivery, what we are seeking is a complete redesign of the process of training the patient to understand when advice is needed, getting the patient to capture symptoms, then connecting the patient with the relevant triage, advice and treatment.

Begins At Home

Implied is a definition of the medical knowledge and equipment that every household should have. This suggests a training program. Do schools currently provide this knowledge. I think not. Can I purchase the training book on what every household should know? Can I purchase the diagnosis kit to generate some insight into the condition and some understanding of the choices for further diagnosis and treatment? Is there an App for that? No, No and maybe.

On diagnosis, if we could capture - at home - a drop of blood, spit, or other emissions to be rapidly sent to pathology for analysis, would this help? I think so. Most maladies leave a trace in the blood, many in the saliva or some of the other bodily juices.

Chat Follows Bloods

Referral to an appropriate practitioner could follow pathology, rather than a 'pot luck' consultation before pathology as now. Can you see the possibility of increased efficiency here? The practitioner with the appropriate skill set is connected with the patient in need of his/her/their skills and provided with the relevant pathology report. Diagnosis may be possible just using the pathology report reducing the time commitment of all parties.

Notice that you are accustomed to giving zero consideration to the time wasted by the patient running hither and yon to get referrals and traverse the ill-designed diagnosis and treatment maze.

Let A Thousand Flowers Bloom

Let us start with training, where do people discover their

knowledge about wellbeing, at school, on the internet, parent courses, from grandma or from their peers. We need a model of how this works now and models for each of the proposed frameworks, so that their merit can be considered.

Or do we need a profusion of possibilities so the natural selection can identify which processes are most effective.

Tweaked For Your Dna

An associated issue is the recommendation of the medical kit that should be present in every house. This kit should contain the normal materials, plus additional materials tailored to the specific needs of each of the members of this household to suit their DNA profile.

Citizens already have some knowledge of symptoms, diagnosis and treatment. Some of this is learnt at home, perhaps from grandmas who grew up in a more self-reliant world. Many families used to have a 'Family Doctor" book to help with triage and treatment. Is there an app for that?

Ideally the app would contain some learning modules and diagnosis modules to help citizens to diagnose and treat some ailments and where required decide which part of the health system to approach.

Farm 10 Billion Bacteria

Did the doctor explain to you that you are a life support system for the 10 billion bacteria that live in your intestine? You are the farmer for this population of beasties. When you drink alcohol, the number of bacteria multiplies. As you sober up the expanded bacteria population are having a death fight in your intestine to see who survives. No wonder you feel a bit crook.

I showed the doctor and old wound with some redness. He said press it, if it hurts it is infected. Didn't hurt, so it is a skin irritation. How come no one had told me this before.

These stories seeking to illustrate the idea that with

more widespread knowledge, the demands on the medical practitioners will diminish and wellbeing will increase.

Triage

Do I call Nurses online, go to my General Practitioner, head to the hospital, call an ambulance, take an aspirin or sit tight till the problem goes away. Most medical problems fix themselves. This is why we have survived for thousands of years. Everyone is better off if the advice is sit tight, your body knows how to handle this affliction.

This approach would have worked well for the under sixties during Covid who did not need to be locked ... was it up or down. This shows that the vast damage inflicted on millions of people was arbitrarily chosen by politicians and was not necessary.

Idiosyncratic

We are on the brink of treatment that is specific to your very own DNA. Ideally the app would contain details of your medical history and your particularities. So the generalised average pronouncements of the doctor may be superseded in favour treatments that are tailored just for you.

We are hoping to design a system that works more effectively to provide each citizen with knowledge, advice and treatment much more effectively than the current system which has arrived by historical accident. How many times have you given a medical history to doctor, where this information should have been available on your file. Redoing the medical history many times is a waste of your time and that of the medical practitioner. One of the design goals of our new system would be to diminish the time wasted on unnecessary, repetitive processes.

The project should consider how services should be grouped and located. For example each group of 200 people should have access to these services, each group of 1,000 people those services and so on up to 100,000. We need a modular design so the elements can be tested, the effective ones kept and the rubbish discarded.

Surely we can design some frameworks for diagnosis and delivery of services that are more effective than the inefficient jumble we have today.

Flexing To Meet Demand

When the West-Gate bridge fell, the hospitals were advised to prepare for an influx of patients. Doctors who were paying attention heard the windows at Royal Melbourne Hospital rattle, so they knew something big had happened and that they should prepare for an influx of patients. Where possible we need to expand this idea to allow the system to prepare for surges in demand. We might even consider how to adapt to a pandemic. The reaction to Covid 19 has been both dishonest and incompetent. We can do much better.

How many ambulances, helicopters and other transport options do we need? Where should they be located? How should they adapt to service peaks in demand. It turns out that 'firies' can get to the heart attack victim more quickly than the ambulance. Most ambulances, most of the time, have a patient inside and are going somewhere. Many firies are waiting for the next conflagration, so they can slide down the pole, get to the patient and keep them alive till the ambulance arrives. We should be impressed, this is cross department co-operation that saves lives.

Firies used to concentrate on putting out the fire. Good thinking. However, in a fire, many people used to die of smoke inhalation. Current practice has the twin objectives of keeping people alive and putting out the fire. Death rate has dived. Well done.

Checklist Manifesto

These are examples of institutional learning. There should be much more of this. Atul Gawande in the 'Checklist Manifesto' tells us how some institutions refine their procedures to deliver improved outcomes. Turns out many surgeons need some prompting to follow procedures.

Have people in our institutions read the 'Checklist Manifesto' and applied the ideas to their affairs? We talk a great deal about 'continuous improvement', it is time to deliver. One problem is that improved systems would require fewer staff, while as we know the public sector only ever increases the number of staff. An issue of incentives again.

We should stroke our institutions when they improve and replace them when they do not. We currently allow incompetent morons to linger. Not a good idea.

Trust

When the dust settles on our Covid misadventure, we may find that many in the medical profession followed the brainwashing of suppliers, rather than seeking to understand the pandemic, therefore delivering unsound advice. Some consumers will be less inclined to trust medical opinion in future.

Shorten The List

Davis advises that: 'Demedicalizing a condition involves a wholesale rejection of the very category, a move unlikely to occur without some powerful pressure from outside medicine itself'. The medical profession offers an ever expanding 'invitation to infirmity'.

Note the tendency for insiders to expand their activity and the need for external intervention to control this wanton expansion.

People Power

Could this basic training in how to keep people alive until the ambulance arrives be widely available at zero cost? Should training in the skills required to drive an ambulance be widely available at zero cost? How many other useful skills that would allow us to flex to meet a crisis should be shared among the wider population.

Perhaps the Country Fire Authority, the local surf club or the Scouts and Guides provide a model. Citizens training-up to deal with emergencies. The passive 'baby sparrow', 'government will save me', approach is pathetic, very expensive and does not flex to meet emergencies.

Self Reliance

There are many, many details to be considered, for example should households who have undertaken the training have lower health insurance costs. My belief is that their costs should be lower as they will access the system less often and in a more efficient manner. If you have the recommended medical kit in your house, lower premiums. If you have the triage app in your phone, lower costs. The principle is that where citizens access the system less often and in a more efficient manner, they should be rewarded. Maybe simply a refund based on lower usage might capture this idea.

People who call the ambulance whenever they sneeze should pay a premium for distracting the paramedics from more important cases. The insurance industry knows how to price these services, if they are allowed some room to move.

Born In A Sauna

We should consult the Swedish, they are very good at collaborating on community issues. Something to do with surviving hard, long winters, often in small scale communities, I suspect. Alternatively, there may be some magic about being born in a sauna.

Recommendation: that the entire health system be redesigned, in a modular manner that will allow evolution, from categories of professionals, training of professionals, training of citizens, availability of pathology, through triage to treatment.

LAW

Civilised And Reasonable Citizens

The Law provides a framework for conventional society, from the constitution, through contract to criminality and functions more effectively in Australia than in many countries. We should be grateful for that.

Ideally people should be able to get on with their life, in a community of civilised and reasonable citizens, most of the time following established conventions and not needing access to the coercive power of the law. Some of these conventions are based on the frameworks provided by the law for conveyancing, contracts, regulation and wills to achieve desired outcomes. Lots of collaboration and cooperation. Where disputes arise the Law or arbitration should facilitate a prompt and economical resolution.

We should minimise the incidence of expensive, slow and unpredictable legal processes. We might look for lower cost, prompt and predictable approaches to disputes, some online approaches are being tested.

Big Abuses Small

Is it possible to diminish the incidence of one citizen using the law to oppress another? What about organisations that oppress citizens, or large organisations that engage in unconscionable behaviour towards suppliers.? Suggest that we have a look to see what canbe done.

Behind The Veil

What can I say? Those of us not working in the law have a very limited understanding of how it all works and are frequently surprised by outcomes. Then newspaper reporting is so ill-informed these days, that one would have to dig into the details of the judgements and even then, many are reversed on appeal. To what extent have our judges become politicised?

Cricket

I have played some village cricket and know that it was a very important part of village life. The pub shut at 2PM and opened again at 7PM, the cricket filled the interval. If their batsmen were falling too quickly, poor bowlers were used, no point in ending the match before the pub was open, a very sophisticated endeavour.

The entire village was involved from Lords to labourers, the young did their courting between innings. I played for Lodsworth in the Ebernoe Horn Fair, the local Lord donated a ram to feed the crowd. The horns were mounted on a plaque and awarded to the player who made the most runs, showing some respect for performance. Following the cricket, there were sporting events for children and a feast. Ah … village life.

Karen

A Karen arrives in a village and seeks to use the law to close down the cricket that has been played on the village green for 70 years. This problem could have been addressed by the inhabitants of the village. Imagine that this Karen suffered social ostracism, an appropriate fate. The inevitable outcome would have been that she had to leave the village. While we have all enjoyed Lord Justice Dennings dissenting judgement in Miller v Jackson (1977), the law is not always the answer.

We should consider what might be done with serial complainers, perhaps starting with education and escalating to sanctions. Karens brace yourselves.

Miller's Tale

On the other hand, in Hadley v. Baxendale a satisfactory outcome was delivered. The court garnered some insights into milling, mill shafts, logistics and spare parts, applied the law and life went on. Is it simpler now that we have a regime of proximate cause, contractual allocation of loss and fair disclosure?

Notice that bad induction produces greedy, selfish, uncivilised people, who lack community awareness and set out to use the law to abuse the wellbeing of others. How do private schools rate here?

Improved induction, should produce fewer appeals to the coercive power of the law.

Individual Responsibility

Henry Maine explores the transition from the traditional collective responsibility of a family to individual responsibility under a contract, our current approach. Douglas North advised that, coercive power is needed to deal with contract enforcement and criminality, but should not be widely used to intimidate and subjugate our citizenry. OK, so who provides the feedback when coercive power is misused?

Police bashings of passive citizens in Victoria are apparently OK. We need more work in this space, ombudspersons merely tinker at the edges.

Genuflection To Napoleon

Recently we have embraced 'human rights', a genuflection to Napoleon, bringing European vague pronouncements - liberté, égalité, fraternité - to challenge Anglo Saxon practicality. Now anyone can sue if they have hurt feelings.

What utter nonsense. On this basis everyone could sue everyone else at the end of every interaction. The whinger code,18C should be annulled. The Australian Human Rights Commission abuses its power to accomplish political agendas, and trawls for additional cases, both highly improper. We do not need this commission.

It was interesting to observe Triggs being triggered by the notion that her activities should be subject to review. She imagined herself to rank above the Australian parliament. Maybe the $500,000 salary had a corrupting effect. Paid more than the Prime Minister, clearly more important.

Time to close this nuisance institution and save some money.

Range, Quality, Cost

How do we decide the range, quality and cost of legal services?

What is the process for considering refinement and improvement?

There is some literature available to open up the discussion, let us start with Susskind, Black, Howard, Ferguson and Dickens.

Susskind suggests that of the 17 services delivered by the legal profession only 2 deserve the fat fees that are charged. Research, project management and many other services are available at more modest price points. Major corporations such as Rio Tinto can and have considered these matters, outsourced directly many of the elements of their legal services and reduced their costs. The average Josie or Josh, Mahalia or Ming, the small business owner and private citizen have much less negotiating power and less money than Rio and so must think carefully before embarking upon a legal adventure.

Conrad Black on the Canadian situation: 'The legal profession is the perfect 360 degree monopoly, a cartel of restricted entry where its members in their legislative capacity enact the laws and regulations, in their government administrative capacity impose them, in their barristerial capacity argue them, in their judicial capacity judge the arguments that must of necessity, arise over them'. Further, 'a profoundly corrupt arrangement which is sheltered by … pious claptrap about the rule of law … being all that raises us above the level of the jungle'.

Philip Howard in the United States, declares that, there are so many rules that people and institutions cannot function effectively.

Niall Ferguson muses on the slide from the 'rule of law' to the 'rule of lawyers'.

Charles Dickens in Bleak House published in 1852, suggests that allowing lawyers to prolong cases to increase their fees diminishes the pursuit of justice. Charles might further ask, does the Law exists to codify and reinforce conventions that the citizens value or to create arbitrary thickets of rules to create disputation and prosperity for lawyers?

The challenge is to design a system that helps society function, where the incentives for lawyers are to be useful rather than simply enrich themselves.

Have we designed such a system? The Australian Law Reform Commission should have a role here.

Pretend Reform

The Australian Law Reform Commission (ALRC) has the potential to do useful work, in 2019 it proposed a body of work to be approved by the Attourney General. As always in the Gramsci Goon World it included constitutional alteration, climate change and migration in the list of five key issues, while at the same time, claiming to be non-political.

Are these high priorities with the Australian people? The ALRC does not know or care. What is woke is wonderful. The ALRC should not be misleading the Attourney General with this biased political advice.

Demonstrating either an ignorance of, or deliberate misrepresentation of the meaning of online surveys with self selected participants, the ALRC claimed that Australians approve of the current volume and composition of migration. This survey did not sample the opinions of Australians. Before making claims about migration, sound research should be undertaken. The ALRC does not have these research skills, however they felt free to make unsupported assertions about migration.

You have violated your charter by straying into the area specifically reserved for decision by the parliament.

More Gramsci Goon politics by a government funded body. Explain to me why immigration was limited for people from France, Chile and many others while in the same year 100,000 came from China. Seems a little unbalanced, non?

Violation Of Charter

In August 2021 the ALRC chose to censor a submission to its enquiry into judicial impartiality. A serious well documented, well-argued submission from a respected think tank directly relating to the topic of the enquiry was blocked from publication because the ALRC chose to assert that it 'contained material that is defamatory'. The political biases of the individuals at this publicly funded body determine what can be published. This is a violation of the charter. The ALRC should be closed and the members charged with violating the charter of the organisation.

Open Mike

Hon Michael Kirby AC CMG mused that reform of the law is 'too important to be left to the experts'. Perhaps we could ask parliament to nominate a commission of elders to consider how the law might evolve to create a more practical and economical framework for both governing behaviour in society and rapidly resolving disputes.

You may be aware that individuals who can rise above self-interest are rare. Identifying them is also difficult. Nevertheless, progress depends upon finding such people and listening to their recommendations.

Recommendation: That the Australian Law Reform Commission be recognised as a bureaucracy that is not fit for purpose and replaced by commission of elders nominated by parliament.

The Shape Of Barristers

Barristers come in all shapes and sizes, with a range of life experience, knowledge bases, biases, attitudes and BMI. Clearly well fed. What about exercise? That is physical exercise, the neurons will look after themselves, washed fresh every night, 'To sleep, perchance to dream'.

Professional Gambler

I knew a barrister who had in earlier careers been a money market dealer and a professional gambler. Seemed to me that this numeracy may have attracted some clients. Julian, let me know how it went.

Sound Advice

Best money I ever spent was for twenty minutes with a divorce barrister, the advice suggested that staying out of court was a good idea. There were 52 judges in the marital jurisdiction, each with their own idiosyncratic approach, it was a lottery, unless your barrister could find a cause for delay, re-throw the dice and get a different judge allocated. We managed to settle before having our day in court.

Expensive, Acrimonious, Uncertain Outcome

A friend of mine when considering legal action against ex-partners after the dissolution of an architecture partnership was advised that many legal firms are set up to handle major disputes between large organisations and therefore have a very fat fee structure. So an action would be very expensive, acrimonious, with an uncertain outcome. He took the advice and got on with his life. Notice that this approach allowed the jerks to flourish. Is this how to build a civilised society?

Jack The Jerks

Could we create a legal test 'does this decision allow jerks to flourish'?
Anecdotes can be amusing, however, we seek to open pandora's box and consider the how we might better connect the law to the social conventions that enable the functioning of our society.

Integrity And Efficiency

Ask a law firm if their recommended standard terms of sale, were matched with their standard terms of purchase could a transaction take place? If not, why not? Are we just seeking revenue here? Is this an ethical issue? I think so.
Is the goal to help the world function or just to end up in court?

Adversarial Obsession Not Universal.

Robin Montano was the in-house lawyer when we were discussing the Heads of Agreement between the British Government and the Digital Equipment Corpoation, he sought find words that expressed the agreement between the parties. Don't be shocked, the adversarial obsession is not universal. All clauses agreed except the pricing clause. We never did reach agreement, however, we maintained the machines, they paid the bills, life went on just fine.

Tickle Me

The Mason supreme court discarded the feathers and went for the whole chook, appointing themselves to make laws, rather than restraining themselves to their actual role of interpretation and application of the law. Pierce avers that the Mason supreme court became politicised, inferred constitutional implications and weakened 'stare decisis' the respect for precedent.

People Like Us

Lawyers are people, just like us, who serve their own self interest when they can. What is to be done? We have tried letting them self-regulate. It does not work. Who can constrain their expansion and monitor their conduct? Does Parliament have this responsibility.

Perhaps we should prohibit the entry of lawyers in to parliament as it is a conflict of interest. People who profit from the creation of more laws should not be given the opportunity to create more fee-generating occasions for themselves and their friends.

Recommendation: Lawyers be prohibited from entering parliament.

Efficiency, Relevance

Where is the pressure on the legal profession to serve the wellbeing and prosperity of the citizens, limit its own size and fees, improve its efficiency and relevance? There is very little.

Happy Productive Citizens

Laws do not make a great society, citizens do. Most people, most of the time, are getting on with life without the need to consult lawyers. The law is available to provide coercion at the margin. Society would come to a standstill with high volumes of legal disputes.

If the citizens do not know how to behave in a civilised and productive manner, then we need to improve our initiation processes and relationships. Imagine that we had an induction process that helped all citizens learn how to live together in a happy and fruitful manner, encouraging collaboration and diminishing the number of misunderstandings and disputes.

Induction

This induction process should be applied to all refugees, immigrants and visa holders. At one time we were allowing car hire for tourists who did not know on which side of the road to drive. May have some serious consequences.

Wellbeing Of The Civilised Majority.

People who register a company, run it for 11 months, then close it before any tax is due, then start again, should be vigorously pursued. Our current conventions allow too many sly scamsters to prosper. We have already asked for a legal test to 'jack the jerks'.
It is not appropriate to ask for peaceful cooperation from the majority, if we do not aggressively deal with and bring down the thieves and rogues. We should review all aspects of the law to consider how to better protect the wellbeing of the civilised majority. Where the law enables bad behaviour, it must be revised. We can do much better on this project.

Jerks In Mercs

The archaic concept of 'Master and Servant', carrying shades of slavery seems inappropriate in our modern, to some extent, egalitarian world. Perhaps we should be moving towards the German system of having an operating board and a strategic board, with labour representatives on the operating board.
Some employers provide an employee share purchase program to encourage engagement. This could be mandated with some proportion of ownership passing to employees each year. There

is room for some fresh thinking here.

We would prefer that the law did not encourage the obsessives who climb the greasy pole to behave badly. Can we imagine a world with fewer 'jerks in Mercs'.

Affordable, Available, Accessible

We should examine how to make dispute resolution more affordable and more widely available, perhaps through tribunals with specialist knowledge.

The internet is being used to help in the identification of the appropriate service. It is a triage process perhaps analogous to the that used in hospitals. A wider range of services and price points, should enable some evolution.

Perhaps internet based triage insights might be applied in many areas of life, getting the right plumber for example.

Grooming

Most lawyers have limited interest in, or understanding of, the way we groom our young to be happy and productive citizens, they are accustomed to a dysfunctional society with a great deal of expensive litigation and themselves at the pinnacle of dispute creation, nurturing, deliberation and judgement.

Perhaps with better grooming we would have fewer Karens, more civilised discussion and negotiation and a sweeter life. Do we need a Karen re-education program?

Recommendation: Development and distribution of materials designed to help our young, refugees, immigrants and visa holders understand how a civilised society functions and that the way we treat one another determines our quality of life.

What Is The 'Rule Of Law'?

We believe in the 'rule of law'. What is that exactly. Tom Bingham suggests the following:

- the law must be accessible and so far as possible intelligible, clear and predictable;
- questions of legal right and liability should ordinarily be resolved by application of the law and not by the exercise of discretion;
- the laws of the land should apply equally to all, save to the extent that objective differences [such as mental incapacity] justify differentiation;
- ministers and public officers at all levels must exercise the powers conferred on them in good faith, fairly, for the purpose for which the powers were conferred, without exceeding the limits of such powers;
- the law must afford adequate protection of fundamental human rights;
- means must be provided for resolving, without prohibitive cost or inordinate delay, bona fide civil disputes which the parties themselves are unable to resolve;
- adjudicative procedures provided by the state should be fair.

Discussion

There is room for some discussion, lawyers are good at that.

Institutional Evolution

We create institutions to accomplish collectively what we cannot accomplish individually.

It is time to examine the scope, cost and quality of our institutions and make improvements.

PRANDIAL 'PUBLIC SERVANTS'

Abusive Relationship

There exists an abusive relationship between the Public Service and the Productive Aussies. One party generates the wealth and the other party spends it. One party creates obstructions, the other must overcome them. One party has high wages, guaranteed employment and generous superannuation, the other party pays for it, while taking all the risks.

The current crop of 'prandial public servants' have a profound misunderstanding of their role. They feel morally superior, are above the law and receive no penalty for poor service or waste of the citizens time and resources. A fat salary for 30 years of doing not much of value, then another 30 years on a fat superannuation package doing absolutely nothing. Why should we take money from the productive people to fund this bonanza?

Traduced

Headline in the Spectator: 'November 11, 2021: the day the great war against the private sector was won'. 'In the 12 months to end June 2021, the number of public sector employees across the three levels of Australian (Commonwealth, State and Local) government increased by 3% to 2.1 million'. Judith Sloan observed that 'Payments as a percentage of GDP rose to 32.1 per

cent, the highest proportion in the post-war period'.
They cost $183 billion and got a 5% salary increase while the private sector was being destroyed by illegal and ineffective lockdowns. Two trillion dollars in debt and still spending. In Victoria an extra 19,000 public servants and a salary increase of 9%.

Who benefits? The public servants got to buy the houses abandoned by business owners and private sector employees. Does this buy the votes of the public servants? Do they have any idea where the money to pay for this largesse is to come from? Is it sustainable?

Parasite As Prince

It is bizarre that the parasites who prey upon the productive people should imagine themselves to be inheritors of the coercive power once exercised by kings and queens - the parasite as prince/princess/polysimulating (PAP).
The prandial public servants who are supposed to serve, must be taught to keep their place. It is not on top. These parasites must suck less and serve more.

Courageous People Should Flourish

Once upon a time, the courageous people flourished, not any more. In each recession the lives of private sector people are ruined, sell the house get divorced, commit suicide, meanwhile the public sector people award themselves larger wages, buy bigger houses and more expensive holidays. A massive transfer of wealth from the producers to the passengers.
In the long run there will not be any more producers and we will all starve and die.

Bankers Make Thing Worse

During Covid the lives of many Productive Aussies were ruined by government edicts of doubtful legality and efficacy. If they dared to protest they were hunted, bashed, handcuffed and taken away by the political police. Business, marriage and life ruined, they make a distressed sale of their house to a Labor-voting public servant.

Banks as usual engage in positive feedback to make things worse, because we have arbitrarily and mistakenly decided to guarantee public sector salaries and employment, banks will lend more readily to public sector people allowing them to buy bigger houses. Neither bankers nor public servants seem to have realised that their salaries are paid by the private sector.

You may know that systems that survive have negative feedback. Ask an engineer. The atomic bomb is an example of a system with positive feedback.

Share The Pain - All In This Together

As policy, we should decide that the public sector will share the pain in every recession, pandemic or other economic hardship. For example a reduction of pay by 30% and a reduction in number by 10%. Instead governments at all levels have been initiating unnecessary construction projects to feed their followers.

The casual destruction of the lives of the productive people by the cosseted, ignorant and overpaid public servants during Covid must lead to a re-negotiation of the terms of the contract. Atlas reminds us of the cost of lockdowns 'missed cancer screenings, missed surgeries, nearly two years of educational losses, bankrupted small business, depression and drug overdoses, overall citizen demoralization, violations of religious freedom, all while public health massively neglected the actual at-risk population in long-term care facilities'.

Unfortuntely, the Handwashing, Masked, Hermes Scarfed Queen Deborah grabbed the microphone in the run up to the US election and subverting the President, locked the world down.

We will eventually check the data on lockdowns, and discover that they were not effective and therefore not justified.

Value Vs. Cost

For many parts of the 'public sector' it is not clear what value they add.   For example, the states are responsible for health and education, yet there are in Canberra, bloated, very expensive health and education departments, doing what exactly? Fashioning transgender brainwashing for primary school children? Vote buying with vague undeliverable promises? Both departments should be closed.

We should examine the necessity, cost, value and quality of all government activities and question the labour-intensive mode of implementation. There must be some public servants who deliver more value they cost, however if you add in 30 years of very generous superannuation, a very large proportion of the government employees cost more than they deliver.

Burden Of Proof

The burden of proof is on the people whose salary we pay, who work in the public sector to prove that they earn their money. It is not up to us to make the case. You want to live on money taken by force from the productive people, then show that you deliver value.

If you are unwilling or unable to demonstrate that you produce more than you cost (including superannuation) then you should resign. You are a thief. If you have never considered this idea, then that is a moral failure of yours. Please resign immediately and go find a job where you can deliver some value.

Malcolm's Memphis

Can we imagine that there are some public servants who produce more benefits than their cost? Yes, we can imagine that, perhaps 10% of the total number. Perhaps customs officers, nurses and soldiers. If we found this to be true, we should keep these useful ones and discard the others. How do we identify them? To address this issue in a 'Yes Minister' idiom, the public servants would advise the hiring of additional public servants to consider this matter.

They performed this scam on Malcolm Fraser when he sought to reduce costs by amalgamating universities. They created an umbrella over the top, using more public servants, so that to Malcolm it appeared that the combination had taken place. This entailed even greater cost. It does not matter what you ask for … the answer is more public servants and more misappropriation of money.

Were these scoundrels punished? Perhaps we should go back, identify them and remove their superannuation. We need parliamentarians who can bring the bureaucracy to order and extract some value.

Spill

NAB at one point required all of its 300 senior managers to re-apply for their own jobs with young, very expensive McKinsey theorists advising who should be retained. Curious that NAB needed outside advisors to work out which managers were competent. Maybe Frank (the teller who got lucky) just wanted to frighten his subordinates.

However, in the public service, after the spill, outside advisers will definitely be needed to help decide who delivers value and therefore who should be rehired. You wanted private sector pay rates, now it is time for some private sector rigour.

Recommendation: all Federal Public Service jobs be declared vacant with all of the millions of place-holders required to justify why money should be taken from the productive people and given to them. If you cannot show what value you deliver to the productive people then there is no reason to pay your salary. Go and find a real job.

Storm Troopers

This especially applies to the Stalinist Storm Troopers from the Australian Bureau of Statistics who harassed and threatened me on my doorstep and would have ruined my life with excessive fines if I had not submitted to their imperious command to participate in one of their surveys. Really, Australians cannot choose to not participate in a survey?

Since when can some self-important government official cancel the rights of a citizen? I contacted my local member who referred the matter to the minister. The minister became part of the problem when he claimed that citizen abuse was OK.

All of these fascists should be caned, imprisoned, perhaps exiled, they do not belong in Australia.

Mr K.

In the Keating 'recession we had to have', how difficult was life for the so-called 'public servants'? Check this - the Ministry for Foreign Affairs was spending $250,000 on a barbecue facility for the lunchtime use by its staff in the middle of the recession. How much did the Weber kettle in your backyard cost?

Meanwhile productive small business people were losing their business, their house, their marriage, their children and their life. Pleasure for the parasites, persecution of the productive who paid for the barbeque.

It is time for the 'recession we had to have' logic to apply to the public servants, we cannot afford them. We are 'all in this together', now it is your turn. Look at the damage inflicted on the private sector during Covid, it is now time for public sector workers to share the pain. One more time, 'we are all in this together'.

Size Matters

The government one hundred years ago was a tiny octopus not doing much damage, now the government is a giant Kraken - ten times larger - squeezing the life and joy out of the productive people and the economy.

Our politicians did not seek and therefore did not receive approval from we the voters to expand government activities to this extent. Let me repeat, government expenditure as a proportion of total expenditure has multiplied ten times. This unauthorised vote buying splurge must be reversed. We cannot afford the wages of these prandial public servants, let alone their superannuation.

Public servants who want their superannuation to be paid should vote for a reduction in their own numbers. I know that you believe in magic mushroom economics, however listen up we cannot afford you. It is in your interest to get these numbers down.

Lop Some Kraken Limbs

Ronald Reagan advised that: 'No government ever voluntarily reduces itself in size. Government programs, once launched, never disappear'. Parkinson declared that government departments increase in numbers without any regard to mission or outcome. Let us hope that both Ronnie and Cyril were wrong and that we can lop some limbs, get the Kraken's thieving tentacles out of our pockets and release the squeeze.

One century ago people were self-reliant and resilient, now there are many who expect the government to buy their vote with government largesse and replace the traditional role of husband, by delivering both money and protection. We need a smaller and much cheaper operation, more squid than Kraken.

We also need more voters who ask themselves where does the money come from? The fantasy of a vast bucket of government money so that we can just spend and spend is delusional and will lead to disaster.

Tutti Fruiti

To help public servants adjust their arrogant attitude and learn to serve, we should command them to be fruit pickers for three months each year, solving two problems with one policy, getting in the fruit and getting the public servants to do something useful.

We might need to bring in the army to ensure that the public servants get up, get to work and perform to a satisfactory quality standard. They are accustomed to being very well paid, while doing very little, with zero penalty for poor performance.

Do you remember when the Bureau of Statistics screwed up the census? This clown did not realise that people might log on on the Tuesday night, so the system crashed. Clearly both irresponsible and stupid. Did anyone get sacked? Let me know.

Parliament Of Mothers

Mothers are the most important people in our community. Society exists to provide support to mothers. We are looking for advice on how to recognise and support this vital role. Without mothers our species goes extinct.

We should ask them how we might better support this role, for example, would paying a salary, providing a house and funding superannuation be helpful. Whatever it takes. A parliament of mothers to fashion some advice for policy makers. We need to keep the simple-minded shriekers away. This is a serious business.

The low birth rate shows that we are on the way to extinction. If you do not have a child you are committing suicide. Please help us to understand your situation and help us to find better policies.

Cruella De Ville

Members of the beautiful gender understand better than any bloke, that being a female in our modern society has an immense range of choice and a multiplicity of roles. In the work force, you can 'Cruella de Ville', Miranda Priestly, Florence Nightingale, Lara Bingle, Gail Kelly, Margaret Thatcher or Kylie. Other roles include, best friend, sporting jockette, party animal, dancing queen, Karen, carer, spiritual adviser, teacher, learner, lover, pussy hat wearer, diva, too many choices. It is your life, do your thing.

How many blokes understand women? Maybe the husbands that understand and follow the maxim 'happy wife, happy life' are getting warm. Buried inside this straightforward maxim is the notion that the family is created by the mother who has a deep understanding of people, society and a commitment to the wellbeing of her brood and that everyone else is in a support role.

We need advice. What we have now is some accident of history, perverted by lots of government interference.

Not everyone supports the notion that your job is the most important thing in life. The current convention of 'pop the kid', hand it off to a poorly paid stranger and get back to work may not be ideal for the kid, the mother or society.

Can you see that there is room for some discussion and consideration of new approaches. May I say again, we are looking for advice.

Blokes Optional

If we remove the need to have a bloke around to pay the bills, would that reduce the incidence of domestic violence? I think so. Can you see that counselling and shelters do not solve the problem. Current approaches perpetuate the problem, we would like your advice on how to fix it. We can do much better.

Mothers Rule

How about schooling delivered by mothers, social welfare delivered by mothers, medical triage delivered by mothers, social disputes resolved by mothers. Can you see that we understand that mothers are the most important people and that we think you should take many of the important decisions. Vote us in, we will convene the parliament of mothers and you can tell us how you would like the system to run.

Mothers could replace many of the public service roles where these issues are poorly and very expensively administered and perpetuated.

Prandial Pride

In their proud Canberra Public Service asylum, economics, business, trade, technology, power management, water management, exports, security and defence are optional, artificial abstractions. Given that they do not understand these matters, we must take charge and bring the system back under control. Credit where credit is due, they are doing a great job on the 'gay marriage' chimera.

Sweet Life

Then there are the unproductive work practices, if you linger in the office 5 minutes past 4.55PM, you get an extra 5 minutes of annual leave. Public Sector Unions have been very successful in garnering for their members a wonderful lifestyle where you do not have to do anything useful, are very well paid, are above the law, stay on full pay through recessions and pandemics, suffer no consequences for your failures, this includes causing recessions, unnecessary trade disputes, ridiculously onerous regulations, screwing up the census and many more anti-prosperity measures. Life gets better for the passengers and harder for the producers, eventually this will destroy the entire system.

Spending other people's hard earned money is profoundly

corrupting. It is their principal pleasure and cardinal sin. For the record and for the millennials, the cardinal sins are: pride, greed, wrath, envy, lust, gluttony, sloth, sexting and spending.

How Much Is Enough

The question is not how much money do these politicians and apparatchiks wish to fling at their fetishes, it is how much money do we allow them to have. It is our money - not theirs. The government share of GDP is now ten times what it used to be and should be. Improper vote-buying schemes for special interest groups have corrupted both the political parties and the parliament and must be cancelled.

Aphiderous

Picture a little green insect, an Aphid inserting the proboscis into the sap source and filling with juice. Neither farmers nor plants enjoy this process. However, there are 4,400 species in the Aphid family. Being a parasite can be a highly successful strategy, in both the natural world and in our unnatural Molongholistic, asylum for the incontinent and the indolent.
The Aphid Style Public Sector has become bloated to the extent that we cannot afford, they are sucking far too much of our juice and pissing it away on their own fetishes.

Golden Goose

Apparently, neither the public sector unions, nor the members, understand that the Productive Aussies pay for their luxurious party. If you kill the goose that lays the golden egg, there are no more eggs and you starve. This idea has been captured in fables from many countries, over many centuries 'those who have plenty want more and so lose all they have'.
Listen up, the 'magic mushroom money tree' you believe in does not exist. Prosperity is created by the productive people.

Forgive me if this seems a tad obvious, we are dealing with truly ignorant and selfish people here.

If these morons continue on the current track we will not be able to pay their salaries or their superannuation. However the practice with brainless parasites is that they continue sucking blood until the population of hosts declines and then everyone starves.

Smart parasites make sure that they do not suck too much blood, keep the host alive and allow a future for both parties. Is 'symbiosis' the key word?

Seems that the little green aphids are smarter than the bloated, grey public servants.

Unintended Consequences

The reason that most government policies have unintended consequences is that cultures are networks of immense complexity, beyond the reach of the human brain. So policy makers formulate some feel good, vague, vote buying, focus-group tested, simple minded fantasies and seduce the naive end of the voting spectrum. Why vague? So that more of their family members can be employed to administer the confusion.

Wombat Seniority

Who gets the senior roles? Is it based on competence, conformity, continuity, convention, cringing, caressing, connections, longevity, seniority, union loyalty, love of wombats, French clocks or what? It is alleged that politicians review senior appointments in the public service, are they paying attention? How about we bring in some outsiders who understand how the economy works and who care about the welfare of the citizens to decide who gets the promotion.

World War 2 Should Have Finished In Week 3

There was a traffic jam of German tanks, guns, troops and trucks on the way into the Ardennes Forest at the start of World War Two. French air reconnaissance saw it and reported it. I have seen the video. The French Commander in Chief ignored the information and continued to send resources to address the German distraction further North.

If a competent general of any nationality and any age had responded to this information, almost all of the motorised units of the German army could have been destroyed at the beginning of the war. Only 10% of the German military were motorised at this time, they could/should have been vaporised. The war would have been over in weeks instead of years, saving millions of lives.

Weeks before there was an intelligence report of measuring-planks being used in the Ardennes Forest to estimate what size of vehicle could get through. This too should have attracted attention. The Maginot Line held. The possibility of skipping by should have been considered. By the way, 'blitzkrieg' was imagined and documented by a French officer well before the war. Is it all that different to a cavalry charge? Plus ça change.

I hate to be ageist, however would you say that 80 something is getting a tad long in the tooth to be controlling a war? Generals are 'in general' accused of fighting every war as if it was the previous war. Who appointed this geriatric. Did the British know? Why didn't they insist on a competent Commander in Chief? More British incompetence costing Australian lives.

Decisions by government-appointed minions have profound consequences. Why would you send your sons to die in consequence of this profoundly irresponsible and incompetent decision making?

Perfidious Albion

Australians volunteered and travelled half way round the world to fight for a civilised world. Churchill improperly wasted their lives preserving the remnants of empire eg. in North Africa and Egypt. One of the reasons the Americans were slow to engage was that they did not wish to waste their blood and treasure on Churchill's imperial fantasies.

Experts

Mao had his so-called 'Great Leap Forward', Stalin dealt with the 'Kulaks', Pol Pot dealt with the intellectuals in each case millions of people died. Let me be explicit, these were deliberate policy decisions that led to suffering and death on a massive scale.

The Mayor of New York moved large numbers of infected people out of hospitals into nursing homes, greatly increasing the spread of the virus and the death rate. Captain bluster, Mr. D turned a quarantine attempt into a super-spreader event, killing 801 people. The victims thought that they were safe in a professionally conducted quarantine. The court case is pending.

Barely mentioned is the real fear that we may have created an Mrna pathway that can wipe out most of our species? Those that had the jab anyway. Ferals tend to survive such convulsions.

More and more people have realised that these 'experts' have feet of clay, and cannot be trusted. This helps to explain the election of Donald Trump, the British retreat from the 'we will regulate everything' fascists and fantasists in Brussels and some jab scepticism.

John Cleese advised that the experts have no idea what they are doing. Sound life advice from the land of 'silly walks'.

Good Information

So called 'Health Experts' in America seem to be controlled by the large number (77 for Pfizer) of Big Pharma lobbyists in Washington DC, access to research funding, bonus payments and the enormous advertising spend. Politicians receive very large donations from Big Pharma. American media is the beneficiary of the massive Big Pharma ad spend, 74% of revenue in the case of Fox, and one must be careful to not offend the paymaster. Follow the money.

Vladimir Putin and most of the epidemiologists can see that the Omicron variant will deliver mild symptoms and immunity to the world. The epidemic is over. Not for Pfizer who are trying to con the world into more jabs.

7,000,000,000 X $20

Last year's flu jab not so popular, this time they got the hysteria to fever level and scored. The payoff is 7 billion people getting an annual jab with a potion that does not prevent death, may cause disability, does not provide immunity, does not prevent spread, has significant sometimes fatal side-effects and lasts just a few months. Multiply 7 billion by 20 dollars and you can see how Big Pharma can afford the bribery listed above. Perhaps you can see why it is difficult to get good information on immunity, ivermectin, side effects and efficacy. We used to trust our 'T' cells. The immunity delivered by a mild brush with Covid is more effective and longer lasting than the recent untested potions. Maybe the 'Omicron' variant is the answer. Mild symptoms long lasting immunity.

Fda Scams

The FDA wants to delay access to Pfizer testing data for 50 years. This is surely criminal collusion. Is it true that the chief of the FDA is a director of Pfizer?

Alexandra Marshall on twitter @ellymelly has tried to help the policy makers get a grip. They are not listening.

Back To Oz

We have our own apparatchiks who have inflicted massive unnecessary suffering through deliberate, deeply flawed policy decisions, informed by ideology (racist selection of contractors), ignorance (no idea where the money comes from to run an economy), incompetence (Turning quarantine attempts into spreader events), fantasy (imagining that the virus can be eliminated) and endless self congratulatory blather.

This latter element demonstrated by the capacity to mesmerise and terrify both the media and the citizens, to accept illegal 'house arrest' and curfews, in order to distract attention from their own role in causing 801 deaths. However, their propaganda unit has found a way to spin all of this so that the gullible still chant 'Istandwithdan'.

These are poor decisions with serious consequences. Cuomo has lost his job. So has his brother. When will Mr. D's time come?

What about 'blond tips', the slug man, who created new arbitrary crimes, instructed police to assault passive people in the street, then on a whim, created heavy fines for anyone who did not immediately grovel.

Samurai

Reminds me of the Samurai who lopped the head off anyone who did not put their face in the dirt immediately. Are we regressing here?

Power corrupts, create a Fuhrer and see what has happened.

Some medical fascist authorising police bashings of passive citizens. Surely he must end up in gaol?

Zero Covid

Perhaps medically trained people should stay within their area of competence, rather than destroying our society. Oh, their advice about medical matters was unsound and frequently changing. The lockdown in pursuit of 'zero covid' was ridiculous and unscientific, yet it inflicted immense damage on millions of people. Does medical training include insight into the economic and political consequences of gestapo style edicts?

Scott Atlas has documented the details of this story in 'A Plague Upon Out House'. I recommend it.

And one more thing, one of the reasons that hospitals are short-staffed is that hospital workers have been seconded to the jab sessions and many are on arbitrarily long quarantine exclusions. Also quarantine eligibility and duration have been optimised to maximise disruption and increase fear.

Just Like The Flu Of 1957

Did medicos check our experience with the flu of 1957? Did the modellers explore the possibility of protecting the over 60s and allowing the under 60s to get on with their life? OK, so go back and model it. You may find under that scenario, that the under 60s developed a superior immunity to that conferred by the experimental potions, had few serious medical problems and their lives were not ruined by unnecessary lockdowns.

Lord Sumption advises that we have managed medical issues of this sort many times before without ruining the lives of billions of people. The lockdowns and 'gestapo' tracking of people were not needed, not appropriate and not legal. More money wasted and citizens crushed.

Most of the Covid damage was created by unsound government policies.

Not My Responsibility

We have all experienced the 'run around' from these puffed up princelings/princesses/pronoun people, 'not my department, you must go somewhere else, we are closed today, our useless internet service is not working again'.

Imagine that Government services were made available at the convenience of the citizens, not the convenience of the insiders. I know that this seems bizarre and exceedingly unlikely. However, we pay their salaries, they are called public servants, what is wrong with expecting some service?

Real Service Delivery

What if, at hundreds of locations across the country, perhaps run by local sub-contractors, all government services were readily available in one location, at one desk, so that a citizen who wants to form a company, engage in overseas trade, open a school, import or export products, join the army or any other useful activity should be provided free advice, support and all the access and information required. All of these requests to be monitored for both response time and customer satisfaction. Notice that the customers are the regulators and evaluators of this service. Servants should serve.

The service pattern should be analysed by statisticians to discover where the bottlenecks are so that we reform the rules or add resources as appropriate.

Public servants rated like Uber drivers, perhaps with similar penalties.

Oh, there are too many different government intrusions into the lives of productive people to make all of these services available from one front desk. That crystallises the point. By forcing the delivery of all services from one front desk we will realise that the government must rationalise its interferences with the citizens and dramatically reduce both their number and complexity.

Run Around

In order to get this service delivered we may need private agents to ensure high levels of service. To be clear, at every location, let me repeat, at every location, all of the public services will be readily available, not in one town, one building or one office at the convenience of the insiders, but at the front desk of every one of these hundreds of offices. No run-around from department to department. No 'I don't handle that'. Prompt, comprehensive advice and service on all matters to do with the government at every front desk.

As a corollary we should upgrade every system of internet access to government information or services, so that it is reliable, easy to use and triggers a conversation with a public servant whenever the citizen wishes. If no front desk people are available then the call will go to one of the upstairs people who must all be trained to deliver this service and evaluated for the quality of their service. You chose to be a public servant, then you must learn to serve.

We do not want crappy service with some refuse-nick public servant hiding behind the power of the government and saying 'no, not me, call later' or just hanging up. We have already had too much of that. Do these people have a 'conscientious objection' to doing useful work?

Public servants who do not help citizens get what they want should be immediately dismissed.

Implementation ... Actually Doing Stuff, Ugh

We have established that much of the advice is unsound and a waste of money, what about implementation, is the quality of implementation improving? I think not. Remember 'pink bats', 'cash for clunkers', 'Covid 19', Seasprite helicopters and much more.

Haven't heard of the 'Seasprite Saga'. We bought 50 year old helicopters - already this story is absurd. Most were in Museums. Worse still, they were designed for non-combat operation dropping a wire with a microphone attached, into the water to detect the presence of submarines. We then tried to turn these museum pieces into combat choppers. $4 billion of money taken from the productive people and dropped down the black hole for less that zero result.

Mincing Poodle

It is almost as bad as planning to build noisy, short range, very expensive, obsolete, easy to find and kill submarines that would not be available till decades after the war. From the politicians point of view, this achieved a few votes for the 'mincing poodle', so no problems.

Malcolm (with the best gilded mirror and biggest ego), you had your chance and screwed it up, it is now time to put a cork in it and let us get on with fixing up the mess you left behind.

Cock Up

Were these policies well thought through, or the usual government blunders with unexpected consequences? It seems that whenever the government has to do something, it is a 'cock up'. Yet we still pay the fat salaries, fatter superannuation and nobody gets sacked. A particular skill of public servants is explaining why the failure 'is not my fault'.

Were the consequences unexpected because of the complexity of the policy space, because the advisers were not up to the task, or is it just that public servants are incompetent? Meddling with the social fabric of society is certainly complex, however we should also consider the lack of life experience this cosseted cohort brings to the table.

Do we need the innumerable - thousands of - Quangos and other government funded hangers on, no we do not. Large savings available here.

Thought Bubble

Currently some moron in parliament has an ill-considered thought bubble - 'there are votes in disability' - the public servants translate the idea into thousands of jobs and more obstructive regulations, leading to higher tax for the productive people. Always adding staff and regulations. What is the process for reducing the number of people and the scope of regulations?

Job Creation

Julia, the Emily List Grandeuse, from an empty house in Werribee (we saw the kitchen, but not the bedroom, maybe some Trade Union trophies there, speak up Bruce), as she slid back into anonymity had two thought bubbles, one about disability and the other about schooling. The first is now costing $25 billion per year and in the other spending has vastly increased as learning has diminished. Scomo serving Julia, who would have thought?
The NDIS has been a job creating jamboree. We cannot afford to continue in the current trajectory. What proportion of the money goes to the disabled and what proportion to the army of public servants? 70% of Julia's billion dollar set up cost for the NDIS went on offices, salaries and navel gazing.

Super

The cost of the exotic and very expensive public servants superannuation program is heading for $300 billion. Yes, you heard correctly $300,000,000,000. It is to be paid for by the productive people in society, much of it falling on our young people, who are locked out of the housing market already, and owe tens of thousands for unnecessary schooling. What? The public servants have awarded themselves $167 billion as at 30 June 2021, rising to $282 billion in 2050. Not 'net zero by 2050' but '300 billion by 2050'. Sound catchy?
This theft is unsustainable and must be remediated.

Public Service Recruitment

Who gets to have one of these very privileged, highly paid,

immensely powerful (above the law) roles? Do the children of the current bureaucrats get preferential access to these jobs? Like European Royalty, are they are marrying their cousins to maintain power. A nepotic self-selected superior class. Watch for an outbreak of haemophilia or something socially or incestually transmitted.

Many spend their lives in 'Byzantium on Molonglo' a fantasy land where you spray other people's money on any daft scheme that comes to mind, with zero accountability for for the quality of the policy or the effectiveness of the implementation. So did their parents. A universal 'basic/exotic income' for generations of a 'passenger class' who do not deserve their privileges.

Diversity, Inclusion, Sustainability

In future all government jobs must be advertised to all citizens not just the inbred Molonglos. The job specification must be written by someone outside the public service, otherwise they will scam the job description to give the job to their cousin. Most of the HR and PR roles are not needed, so there is an immediate saving.

We need some actual Equity, Diversity, Inclusion and Sustainability.

Send A Centurion

In Ancient Rome centurions were promised a plot of land at the conclusion of 15 years of military service. So at the age of 30, they had a farm, could get married and raise a family. Perhaps we should be looking at something similar. Can you see a theme here? If you hope to be considered for a government role, first serve your country. Don't want to serve your country, then you will not be considered for a government role.

Slaves

You would have thought that the prandial public servants would have wished to cancel the Covid lockdown, so that the slave classes of the population - you and me - could slave away to generate the funds to pay for their generous salaries and obscenely generous superannuation. It would seem that this parasite class has no idea where the money comes from - that it may run out - and that their decisions are damaging the productive people's capacity to generate the funds that pay for their public service self-pleasure party.

Kill The Plague

This plague of public servants are like locusts, they are destroying our lives by consuming everything in their path, including our prosperity, freedom and happiness.

Public servants who want their superannuation to be paid should vote for a reduction in their own numbers. I know that you believe in magic mushroom economics, however listen up … we cannot afford you. In order to pay your superannuation we must reduce the number of parasites. Alternatively we could cancel your superannuation.

What about making this generous public service superannuation available to all citizens. That would increase equity. You believe in 'equity' right?

Party Funds

In the private sector, the government mandated 9% superannuation is deducted from the salary, reducing the take home pay of workers and reducing their life choices and chances. Then the finance industry take 30% of the deposits in fees. Another scam that needs investigating and remediation. What about a refund of these illegitimate fees.

In the public sector 14.5% superannuation is paid on top of the salary. This money is then invested with a union controlled superannuation fund. The superannuation funds then cycle the money back to become a donation to the Labor Party. Another scam using public funds to support one political party. Is this democracy? The Labor Party creates very large numbers of highly paid government jobs, pays 14.5% extra for superannuation, gets the money into union funds, then gets it back as donations. Does this violate the laws on political party funding?

Scomo will fix it. Oh, sorry, he is on his knees in front of the climate gods, goddesses and pronouns, and is busy appointing lefties to key roles.

Time to stand up Scomo, that is if you have a spine.

Gramsci Goon March

Unfortunately, we have allowed parasites, preeners and popinjays to populate the parliament, the universities, the so called public service and many more institutions. The Happy Aussies were busy having a life, while an underserving, unqualified and unsatisfactory string of clowns have performed the 'Gramsci Goon March' and taken over our institutions. Is this the ultimate consequence of the Catholic Schools targeting the public service entrance exams two generations ago?

Kkk

Marx, Popper and Lagerfeld, what a team, must be something we can learn here. The English are obsessed with 'class' issues. Marx, writing in London, picked up this vibe and structured his analysis around class. He did his rabbinical scribbling in poxy, pluvious, polluted London while the desperate underclass were starved, abused and exploited, then exiled to the other side of the world. Karl correctly saw that the amoral, kleptocratic, capitalist monsters in London deserved the guillotine.

Karl wanted to end the capitalist world where bad people flourish and good people serve. However, Karl's recipe did not work at national scale. Scale up from tribe to nation and you find that the number of whingers, passengers, scammers, rent seekers, liars, cheats and scoundrels increases exponentially. Village/tribal conventions do not work at the scale of a nation, ask any Russian oligarch, or even Vladimir the Great himself.

Karl should have come to Australia to see proletariat at play. Lachlan Macquarie launched the open invitation Spring Racing Carnival in Sydney in 1810. We created the most egalitarian country in the world, without the overhead of Stalinist repression … until now.

Lose Their Chains

What Karl did not see was that the centralised bureaucracy he advocated would liberate a different set of monsters and lead to dislocation, death, and failure. He dreamed of the time when the proletariat would lose their chains.

In 2021 Australia, Covid has been used as an excuse to put all Australians in chains. Who would have thought - freedom loving Aussies locked in their houses - while police patrol the streets arresting an old lady for sitting on a park bench and a pregnant mum for having an opinion.

Popper

Popper advised that democracy is not the process of giving infinite power to emperors, more correctly it should be understood as an error-correction program where people who make bad decisions are discarded.

Lagerfeld

This Karl has given the best ever description of 'what women want', he did not however mention politics or manifestos. My preference is the 'adore to be adored', 'love to be loved', 'need to be needed' schtick, he is into bubble baths and bottomless credit cards. Your choice.

Another K

Nikita Khrushchev 60 years ago...."Your children's children will live under communism. You Americans are so gullible. No, you won't accept communism outright; but, we will keep feeding you small doses of socialism until you will finally wake up and find you already have Communism." Was he correct?
We do have 'the terror', people hiding in their houses so that they can avoid being bashed by the police. Communism eventually imploded, dare we hope that something similar will happen to our home-grown fascists?
Alternatively, we could do something about it.

Propounding Paradoxes

The paradox is that, after the clear failure across the world of the communist fantasy, the Gramsci Goon March through the Australian institutions has been very successful and some of our half-educated, pseudo-elite are worshipping Karl's discredited ideas. In Australia, we have gone from a strong and self reliant populace to mumbling imported mantras and begging for handouts.
We are the frogs who have been slowly boiled in the Gramsci pot. It is now time to jump out of the pot, before we are completely cooked.

'F' For Fascism, Fail, Flip And Firm

You would have thought that the failure of the '-isms' of last century, Fascism and Communism, might have caused these amateur policy-tinkerers to be careful in their ill-considered proposals. Apparently not, we continue to have clumsy social-engineering experiments foisted upon us.
The concept of gender has been flipped, so that it is determined by whim, we have girls with penises and boys without, could

be confusing, especially after dark. We might reverse the 'look don't touch', to 'touch don't look'. Get a firm grip on 'reality'.

Grab Control Or Allow Cultural Evolution?

It is the violence-based central governments and their apparatchiks who grab control, force decision-making to the centre, disable adaptation and dictate pronouns. Whatever happened to the democratic exploration of ideas and memes?

We need wiser and more modest policy makers. The people will choose what cultural memes are useful and broaden their adoption. Government coercion is not appropriate in these social matters.

Turchin describes this as 'cultural evolution'. It has been operating forever. Our tribal ancestors flourished because they identified new and better ideas, adopted them and preserved them in the tribal group memory. We do not know about those who did not adapt, as they have disappeared. No room for a 'predator in a palace' plundering the people.

Acemoglu and Robinson in 'The Narrow Corridor' speak of finding the pathway between allowing elites to do their exploitation and allowing citizens to have their freedoms. One hundred years ago we were on track. It is time to recover our navigation skills.

We ask voters to review their recent experience and vote for much less government meddling in our lives in the future.

Late Night Whispers

The Socialist Left advised me in the late 1980s that they had a program to populate every - let me repeat every - committee in Australia with lefties, to move the culture permanently to the left and ethically cleanse the unbelievers. They have been immensely successful.

The thesis in this essay is that we must restore some balance.

Gardening

We Aussies can find better ways to share the prosperity created by scientific and technological advances. Do the people who create the technological advances do well? Do the reliable, responsible people who do the work to keep our country running, flourish?

How does it make sense to give so many of the prizes to the middlemen, cheats, chancers, bankers and other parasites? We can certainly do a much better job of dealing with the thieves and rogues who flourish in our poorly tended garden.

Some heavy pruning is needed, get rid of the weeds and keep the tomatoes, potatoes, roses, daisies, apples, oranges and passionfruit.

Policy implementation frequently incompetent. What exactly do we get for the vast expenditure on public servants? If it is not policy and not implementation, what is it? We should liberate these passengers so that they can find a useful role in society. No more luxuriant, lazy, weedy leaves, we need more fruit and veg. Who will wield the pruning shears, we will.

Recommendation: Every government service is provided at hundreds of locations across Australia, with every request being logged and public servants who do not provide rapid, useful response being immediately sacked.

Recommendation: a spill of all government jobs. Apply for your old job and we will consider if you deliver more value than your salary plus superannuation. If not you will be recycled to deliver equity. In a sustainable world, only useful people get paid.

PUSTULE OF POLITICIANS

Galahs

Unfortunately, a parasite class have weaseled their way into power and are destroying our way of life, with excessive preening, preaching, regulation, spending and taxation. In the land of the galah, you can expect some shrieking, the loudest in the gallery, being the shriekettes: Wongster, SHYster, and Lady Tanya, not a useful idea between them. Bring back the 'Supremes', at least they could sing.
How about Kylie for Prime Minister? No more 'White Supremacy' we need 'Girl Supremacy'. I am watching 'The Queens Gambit' and can see that the girls are making their move (PQ4).

Paradise

Imagine Penny Wong, Sarah Hanson Young and Tania Plibersek, did I say 'The Shriekettes' - in paradise, in milk-maid costume, plus tiara, bijou partout, milking the cows by hand every morning and evening, churning the butter by hand, plucking the chooks, erecting fences, tilling the soil to grow their own veggies, making jam, preserving fruit, in short doing something useful, rather than just yapping in parliament. Skip the breeding bit, we do not want more like them and who would bother.

Privileged Princesses

My grandmother, mother and sister had these skills. These parliamentary, privileged princesses might even learn to have some respect for productive people. Probably not. Their usual response to ideas not on their hymn sheet is a brainless ad-hominem shrieking.

You want to live a alternative style of life. No problem. Your friends are in the hills behind Byron Bay, go and join them. However, you will not be using our money and lecturing us in the downstream media.

Integrity From Germs

Aspire to the integrity level of Germaine Greer who bought a farm and restored it to rainforest. Green politicians should learn to engage with the environment, rather than just posturing and lecturing us about it.

Repetitive, Vacuous Clown

Oh, and the heavily frowning, little whinger Albo who has only one idea, that he struggles to remember, that is why he is frowning, it is that everything is Scomo's fault. Was he elected? Why do the media give air time to this repetitive, vacuous clown.

Coup De Grace

Are the lefties in the media trying to engineer another coup? Of course they are, and they are proud of it, the previous one and the next. They even recycle mendacious Malcolm and the reddening Ruddster, hoping that the bitterness of these two failures will inflict some damage and pervert the outcome of the next election. Can we look forward to Kevin 27? When will Malcolm be back, 2050 perhaps? Will it be for the Labor Party or the Greens? After all, like Keating, Malcolm learnt his skills from 'Nifty Nev'.

The labor party could not get elected without the ABC sponsored Greens, this in part explains our lurch to the left.

Journalistic integrity ... pffft.

Annie Get Your Gun

Anne Applebaum reminds us of the nightmare where the bad guy is on top, the cops bash people, most people cringe and a few brave souls try to set it right. We plan to have nice, hard-working, useful persons in positions of influence, so they will be working with you to create the civilised world in which we would all like to live.

Lose The Lurkers

Lurking in the corridors of power is not, and should not be used as, a qualification for entering parliament. Another case of insiders pleasuring themselves at our expense. Costello got Kelly O'Dwyer into Higgins, perhaps we could have undertaken a wider search. This is after all the seat occupied by both Harold Holt and John Grey Gorton.

Peter could not get the support of his own party to become Prime Minister, difficult then, to see how he could have secured the votes of the nation. As Johnny said, 'if you want the crown, you must come and take it'.

Country Ruled By Johnny Walker

Gorton was a fighter pilot in Malaya and New Guinea, grew oranges on the Murray and may have learnt something about life. Under his watch a nuclear plant and steelworks were planned in Jervis Bay. We should have led the world in electricity generated from nuclear power. Fifty three years later, it is time to make it happen.

We need people who have done things in their life, who have some understanding of what goes on in Australian society and a desire to limit government so that we, the citizens can have a life.

Blather-Filled Bordello

The lurkers on the inside have neither understanding of the need to limit the size of government nor motivation to wield the knife. In fact they live in the bland, blather-filled bordello with endless sly appeasement. We need some surgical clarity.

It is time to take over the pre-selection process, select better candidates and vote them in. Then it will not matter that what used to be the major parties are corrupted by preselecting insiders from their own goldfish bowl as they will not be elected. We can't fix them, so we should flick them.

Bonfire Of The Inanities

Voters, please listen up, you voted for this current rubbish. We cannot fix it until you take your vote seriously and support some candidates who will get out of the way and allow the great future available to Australia. We need a bonfire of the inanities. Suggestion … vote for an independent at the next election, if the ZIT Party does not have a candidate in your electorate.

Ignore all politicians promising to steal and spend more of your money. Small is beautiful, especially in government.

Brains Of A Goldfish

These goldfish politicians seem to be amazed that as they swim around their goldfish bowl, the view is for them ever new and arresting, producing repetitive clichés about climate, gender, diversity, inclusion, and the ever vague sustainability. Brains of a goldfish, that explains the absence of thinking. Cliché, followed by cliché, followed by cliché, round and round forever.

Was there a time when we used to talk about productivity, exports, discoveries, security and the factors that sustain prosperity? We need to ascend the evolutionary tree from goldfish, to lizard, mouse, simian, hunter, gatherer, farmer, philosopher, philanderer, poseur, preacher, lobbyist, diplomat, coven convenor and finally to Plucky Aussie.

Foreign Foibles

What are these sad, imported, vague, confected issues? Try diversity, equity, sustainability, voodoo racism, fear of rain, indiscriminate immigration, magic mushroom economics, gender schmender, and we must not forget the very relevant to Australia, and systematically misreported, George Floyd fentanyl overdose. Did you know that Geoge Floyd and the police officer with a knee worked together on private security gigs? Have you remembered that George Floyd was in the police car, jumped out and was trying to escape? Do you know that Floyd had a lethal over-dose of Fentanyl in his system at the time of the fracas?

Primitive 'Ju Ju'

Our reptile brain stem gives priority to love/hate/terror simplifications, leading to cognitive dissonance and selective perception to support the existing view. The apocalypse-based cults, 'injection mania' and 'slay the unvaccinated' are just the most recent. Who could have imagined that this primitive 'Ju Ju' could dominate in sophisticated western societies, especially resilient, raucus, rambunctious, revelling, Aussie-tralia. We use our sophisticated pre-frontal cortex to find explanations for the fear-driven, heavy stuff coming from our primitive brain stem.

Ejacashn And Universidddy

Julia claimed to be fixing ejacasshnn and universiddddy. How is that going? What about pronounciation, or is it pronunciation? Repeat after me, Julia, 'education … university'.   Again 'education … university'.

This moron was pretending to be our Prime Minister. Not interested in foreign affairs, technology, economics, farming, mining, trading or family, then why did you seek this role? Maybe she just wanted to make a pre-prepared misogyny speech? Then your mission was accomplished. Bravo. Didn't you do well.

Blind Freddy

Blind Freddy would know that if the Great Barrier Reef has survived the climate vicissitudes over millennia it will probably be OK. Not Professor Sandra Harding the Vice Chancellor of JCU apparently. She provides 'strategic leadership (sack disbelievers), advises the University Council on all issues (especially climate hysteria) and represents the University in a range of national and international conformity forums'. Also she got ridd of Peter.

Vote Your Beliefs

The election of Youngkin in Virginia shows that the brainless shouting and smearing by ignorant lefties has lost its power. Many middle class people who live their life in a responsible, civilised and resilient manner, have been voting for shrieking lefties. It is time to align your vote with your beliefs.

Ignorance Is Bliss

Some naive voters imagine that the lefties will create a better world. Please have another look, the lefties do not know how to create anything. Well …except confected outrage on behalf of someone they have not met and do not understand. Their better world includes expensive and intermittent electricity, a collapse of the economy, shitty food and a tax on most pleasures.

Shagging Surveillance

What? You want the government in the bedroom? Will we have to do a 'selfie' while being amourous to get the approval of the outsiders who are watching and who by some magic power get to decide if everything is OK? You may be aware that there is a great deal of variation in how people 'make their move'. However, 'The Game' is a bit formulaic. Whatever turns you on. Do I need consent to take the selfie? A consensual selfie. Does this public display become dogging? What about Louis C. K. getting planted?
Is it a mug shot? Do we need a panoramic view, from toes to nose? Will the heavy breathing fog the lens? At which point in the process do we take the shot? Need a steady/friendly hand. What is the preamble called? Fore and Aft? Hold on .... I'm coming.
Perhaps the censorious, 'missionary' Mr. D at the end of the bed waggling his fat finger. Maybe he could set the exposure, the 'f' reading and tickle the shutter. Has 'blond tips' advised the police on the appropriate penalties and what to do with their truncheons? What about the polyamourous? Is this a super-spreader event, a spraydemic? Seems like 'cock up' to me.
These people deserve to be alone.

Perhaps you can see that careful thinking is required in the development of regulations or any other type of relations? Will this policy help us to increase the birth rate? Frigidity the new fruitfulness.
Better still, keep the government out of the bedroom. The generalisation is that less government interference is better.

Impoverished Living Death

Trigger warning, you are prohibited from watching 'Peaky

Blinders', Tommy may say and do some things snowflakes may not like. It is a movie about a wild-dog gypsy. What do you expect to see?

These infantile morons vote for an arid misadventure devoid of pleasure or information, an impoverished living death. This is your invitation to wake up, get a life and join the party.

Another Incontinent Spraydemic

When lefties are in power they spend all the money in treasury, then borrow lots more, spray it all and leave it to someone else to clean up the mess. Two billion to not build a road, four billion on a desalination plant we do not need or use, vast construction expenditure during Covid, plus assorted extra feel good promises. Notice that in the middle of the vast, unnecessary expenditure on Covid, they are increasing other government spending. All this while posturing as someone morally superior. 'Stupid spendthrift' is a more appropriate epithet.

Sweet Voters

We need our productive people to take a little time to explain how the world works to our sweeter voters. Turns out that the vague, seemingly progressive promises are persuasive for some naive voters. The need to pay for education, health, welfare, plus many other feel good aspirations is not understood and so the naive vote goes to the charlatans making the vague promises, rather than the people who can generate the money needed to pay for the hospitals, schools and so on.

The 'magic mushroom' economics upon which these ignorant social-engineers rely on for their inexhaustible flow of money, does not exist. Productive people pay the bills and should be treated with respect.

If we cannot show our naive voters that their actions have doubled the price of electricity - killing both jobs and grandmas - then, the price of electricity will double again - killing more jobs and more grandmas - leading to the apocalypse these young zealots claim to fear.

Picture these grandmas freezing to death each winter because they cannot afford electricity for heating, because they spent the money on biscuits.

These young, green zealots need to acquire some moral values.

Loony, Lazy, Leftie Lamentations

We have been misled by morons on Mogadon, bringing excessive regulation, high taxes, unfunded, irresponsible government largesse and intensive brainwashing with loony, lazy, leftie lamentations. It is time to recover some balance.

Crash

In every mining boom the politicians - with zero foresight - grab more tax, splash money on their fetishes (Fraser and Gillard come to mind) and set up a crisis for the end of the boom.

The banks intensify the eventual crash by pumping up the bubble, then suddenly turning off the tap. Do the directors of these large banks understand their responsibilities? Perhaps we need to spill these roles as well, see if we can get some directors who can get beyond short term greed to helping Australia flourish.

Bitching

Please allow a pause in the polemic for a bit of bitching. The passengers are bodgy, bloody, bludgers, with Buckley's, buggering the, cockies carnal carnival ... it's cactus, a crack in the clacker, drivel by a dinkum, drongo, dipstick, duffer dribbling down a dead dog's donger.

We need to give these furphyesque, feral, flakes the flick, to facilitate our future fluorescence or is it efflorescence?

Aleksander

Solzhenitsyn in the Red Wheel tells us how attempts to quell the bread riots, led to the police being beaten by the hungry, a mutiny in the army and a rampage. Someone needs to tell Dan to get the economy going again or the desperate may make a move. Dan ruins the lives of millions of people arbitrarily, dismissively and unnecessarily and is then surprised to get some push back. What is he smoking?

Grandmas

One grandma ran a self-sufficient farm in Campbellfield with chooks, house cow, fruit trees and veggie garden and a pantry full of delights, raising 5 children, continuing on after the early death of her husband and the loss of a son in the First World War. Her brother was the member for Gippsland for 30 years. I am sure that he received some good advice about how politicians should relate to voters.

She organised the annual Sunday School Picnic, raising money from the locals and renting the moving van for the children's pilgrimage to Mordialloc for their first view of the sea.

Soldiers from the local military camp on exercise, would pause outside her front gate, the CO knew that there would be fresh scones delivered by my 5 year old mother. We used to work together.

Fashionista

The other grandma was a fashionista at the races with a 'rails bookie' husband, together they operated a bread and cake shop in Footscray. During the depression locals who were a bit short would line up as the shop closed on Saturday to receive free bread and cakes.

At the age of 18 grandpa played football for Footscray, then worked his passage to England to continue his discovery of the world. They did a grand tour of America in the 1920s. This grandmother had severe hearing problems, but never complained.

The first grandma was also at the races, she knew some jockeys and trainers, not sure what she was wearing.

Aunt Mary

My aunt Mary ran a general store (Tangambalanga and Plenty) and operated a farm (outside Wang), all high risk ventures, without ever taking out insurance.

What happened to the courage and self reliance demonstrated by earlier generations of real Aussies? Do we allow the people who 'have a go' to prosper? We do not. Worse, we tax and regulate them senseless for the benefit of the passengers.

Could these three resilient and accomplished women be role models for our contemporary whingeing snowflakettes?

Gratuitous Insults

We live in a very interesting part of the world. We are a middle sized power who should be aiming to get along with, and trade with, everyone. It is most unfortunate that an ignorant, clumsy and arrogant Foreign Minister gratuitously insults our largest trading partner. This blunder has made life very difficult for our winemakers, lobster fishermen and many others.

The current crop of politicians and media mediocrities are worse than a waste of space, they are distracting Aussies from the magnificent opportunities available to us with a modicum of clear thinking and diplomacy from Canberra.

Trade, Timor

Instead of blocking 'live cattle' export based on an ABC program, the government should be facilitating trade. Our Timor misadventure was also based on pressure from the ABC. Our American allies wondered why we would go to so much trouble over something that had so little significance. However they still helped us by encouraging the Indonesian military to let us have our little play.

The government should have been establishing sound working relationships with all of the countries in the world. If the ABC followed its charter, we could all be proud. Now that it has become a party political mouthpiece, its entire cost should be listed in the donations to the left. Then it should be closed.

How come our voters spend all this time in school, yet do not understand that having a prosperous economy allows us pay for all the good stuff. Do they teach 'magic mushroom' economics? Voters, if you put the spendthrifts in power, they will spend all of the money and we will all starve. Please check this out, too many people vote for taking the slippery slide to oblivion.

Angry, Autistic, Adolescent

Do you remember in your late teens when you thought that you knew all about everything? Then you learnt some stuff and grew up. We should not be distracted by the autistic, angry, truant, sweary, child Greta Thunberg, the endlessly repetitive Michelle Grattan, the Emily List Queen Julia, the moronic, yappy Penny Wong or snarky Little Missy SHYster. Add to the list Albo, Shorten and Scomo. Kick them out of parliament, let us see if they can become productive and useful people who deserve a place in our society.

Sending Young Men To Die On The Other Side Of The World

The politicians who sent two generations of young Aussies to die in wars on the other side of the world should review their decision. Think of the contribution these young men could have made to the development of our country.

Did this foreign misadventure take out good guys and allow scum to flourish? To some extent. I met a manufacturer who produced '303' shells during the second world war. He boasted of having created an inefficient tooling of the production process, got the price agreed with the government official, revised the tooling to produce the shells at lower cost, then made very large amounts of money throughout the war. Bravo.

My father on the other hand, volunteered, was a pilot in the RAF and crashed on a mission to Jugoslavia. Too many young men blown away in an English genocidal con job. Aussies given the high casualty roles amounts to genocide.

English Stupidity

The reason the English needed assistance is that they were too stupid to invest in their own army, which was a tiny fraction of the size of the German army. Everyone knew that Germany was preparing for war, however the English policy makers were asleep at the stick as usual. Deeply incompetent decisions from the English elite, then we sacrifice our sons to protect the privilege of these deeply flawed and depraved dipsticks.

Our sons sacrificed to prop up the lifestyle of these narrow-minded, greedy, selfish, one might even say uncivilised elites, manipulating British life for their own glee and ease.

From Fromelles To Aukus

Remember the tragic and completely unnecessary loss of thousands of Aussies at Fromelles, launched on extended open ground, contrary to the war manual, in front of the German machine guns. The Brits had the job of taking out the machine guns, they failed and thousands of Aussies were massacred.

I have heard that at the battle of the Somme, when line after line a allies were commanded to walk towards the German machine guns and be slaughtered, that the German soldiers were shouting at the our soldiers to go back.

We should court-marshal the English officers guilty of both of these monstrous pre-planned murders.

Will AUKUS put young Aussies in the front-line of any conflict that comes up in the region. Surely not Aussies put in the forward trenches again? Genocide anyone?

Rand Paul On America

'Politicians have to learn: money has to come from somewhere. Either we borrow it, we tax people for it, or we simply print the money. Borrowing it obviously puts us further in debt. It puts us further in China's debt. With taxing, Americans endure enough government theft already.

Printing money out of thin air has consequences. When the Federal Reserve prints the money, we increase the money supply which makes the current dollar worth less and less. Our money loses its purchasing power.'

Same in Australia, billions are borrowed and wasted by our politicians on unnecessary government fetishes, with inadequate thought about who will have to pay it back.

Michelle

It is time for a change, 'change we can believe in'.

By the way, Obama thought that this hopey, changey, hooplah was low grade rubbish. Michelle persuaded him that it would work. She was right. One might despair that the voters are so gullible or the media so powerful.

Ned Kelly Had Legitimacy

These clowns imagine that it is OK to take money from productive citizens and blow it on vote buying programs for prandial public servants and other malingerers. The first step is to stop their Ned Kelly style banditry - taking our money by force - to flush on their foolish, phantasmagoric fetishes. Ned had more legitimacy, he was trying to feed a family.

Democracy

Do we live in a representative democracy? Who are the parliamentarians representing? We have seen already that the lawyers in parliament seek to expand the influence and wealth of the lawyers. The Country Party looks after the farmers. Labour is financed by and looks after Union apparatchiks. Greens work for Gramsci and kill jobs and grandmas with high power prices.

Who represents Productive Aussies? We will.

Beware The Lobbyists And Rent Seekers

Alexis de Tocqueville in 1831 was most impressed with the American tendency for citizens to get organised in private associations and get things done. He warned us to beware the lobbyists and rent seekers, who can destroy democracy. They subvert the intended purpose of government - providing opportunity for all - and harness government power to divert our prosperity into schemes that provide illegitimate advantage to their sponsors.

Do you remember the pictures of Calwell and Whitlam waiting in the street, while the apparatchiks 'thirty-six faceless men whose qualifications are unknown, who have no electoral mandate' were meeting inside to decide the policy. Calwell and Whitlam were a delegates, following orders from outside parliament.

How come, if we have known about this problem for 190 years have allowed this perversion of both pre-selection and policy to continue?

A relative of mine advised that one should make your money before going into parliament, as the corruption pressure is immense.

Snouts In The Trough

We have allowed the 'snouts in the trough' people to prosper at our expense. We need much better parliamentarians who wish to, and are able to resist the blandishments of these sly subversives. Pfizer spends more money on lobbying and bribing than it does on the development of potions. It is working well for them, finally a compulsory jab for 7 billion people every year. How about we recycle both the snouts and the troughs.

Useless Idiots

The Federation generation understood that government should be constrained to operate in the interests of the people. Parkinson warned us that the number of people in a government department expands without any regard for relevance or utility. Yet we have allowed this hijacking of our prosperity by a vast army of useless idiots. We should take responsibility for this catastrophe and fix it. We have voted sinners of the both venal and carnal variety into office. We must discard the political class and start again. The are plenty of Aussies who can do a better job than the incumbents.

Poor White Trash

Lee Kuan Yew as Singapore flourished and Australia flatlined, suggested that Australians were on the way to becoming 'the poor white trash' of Asia. Confucian societies believe in and support the family. In Western Society the government seeks to take over the family responsibilities with lectures and largesse, meanwhile destroying actual families. It is not going well. Ask the kids.

Biden's 'Build Back Better' will finally kill the family, with government taking over the funding and security roles once delivered by a dad.

Yew again 'In Eastern societies the main objective was to have a well-ordered society so that everyone could enjoy his/her freedom to the maximum. Parts of contemporary American society were totally unacceptable to Asians because they represented a breakdown of civil society with guns, drugs, violent crime, vagrancy and vulgar public behaviour'.

Nudge, Nudge

If the parliament is superintended by people without a moral compass whose one desire is to stay in power, focus group testing many vote-buying ideas, then implementing the set which maximises their vote, both it and they are vacuous?

'Whatever it takes'. Need 200 more votes in a Queensland seat, no problem we will send 200 Victorians to cast their vote in Queensland.

This means that the policy decisions are corrupted by short term, expedient thinking (pink bats, cash for clunkers, live cattle export ban) and the overall expenditure greatly expanded.

Nudge Units use the latest psychological manipulation techniques to brainwash our citizens. Mr. D had his 'Goebbels unit' test his pronouncements in advance to be sure that they would terrify enough citizens. Create mass hysteria and fear and you can drive the mob wherever you want. Those who resisted have been demonised and bashed by the political police.

Pusillanimous, Prandial

We will not forget that you were happy to destroy the lives of Productive Aussies by locking us in our houses, meanwhile increasing the numbers of, and salaries of, already highly paid so called 'public servants'. We will replace the current generation of pusillanimous parliamentarians and prandial 'public servants' with adults.

Is the collective noun a 'pustule of politicians'. We need to lance it.

Quo Vadis

At federation, we had politicians who were ready, willing and able to consider how our wonderful country might evolve. We must reject the current political class as not fit for purpose and elect people who care about our future.

Got The Bull By The Horns

Some in the political class think that Aussies can only engage in behaviour that is approved by the government. This is the opposite of the truth. We must put into parliament people who understand that the government can only take actions that are approved by the people.

We do not have to put up with their improper inversion of reality. They probably do not understand the heading above, having spent their life in the inner city latte belt - bien pensants - where bovine calibre social engineering is du jour and four legged bovines and methane emissions are unknown. Bovine emissions that is.

We can restore Australia to the glory days when people took responsibility for their own affairs and lived an interesting and fulfilling life. Ayn Rand, Adam Smith, Milton Friedman, Asterix, Obelix, Marge and Lisa Simpson, Skippy and Beethoven, would all look down approvingly and smile. Play Beethoven's fifth and feel the urgency. Perhaps one might follow up with some Barry Tuckwell, John Williams, Sculthorpe, AC/DC or 'Men at Work'.

Aussie Tolerance Betrayed

The traditional Aussie tolerance - 'live and let live' - lets us down when we are faced with intransigent zealots who seek to take control of and ruin our society, the 'live and let live' approach gives these micro-minorities free rein to destroy our way of life.

We have tolerated too much of this. It leads to timid policing and a fear of being called racist causing for example, a failure to investigate persistent ethnic gang rapes of young white girls in Western Sydney.
No more, it is time to act.

Smart Arse

We have traditionally been tolerant of a wide range of thinking, behaviour and speech. You could be a smart arse, short arse, hairy arse, fart arse, tight arse, pigs arse, arse about face, arse wipe or even arsing around, whatever. What you must not do, is tell us which words we can use and which we cannot. This absurd arrogance by tiny pronoun pushing putsch must stop.

Fresh Blood

Let us get some politicians who understand 'live and let live', who will restore our freedoms.

DRUG MONEY

Cold Turkey

Why 'Zero Income Tax'? We must cure the politicians addiction to spending, therefore we must cut off the money drug.

Bugger Off

Democracy is about freedom and choice, therefore we should not tolerate the tax man snooping in our private affairs and taking our stuff. Tell them to 'bugger off'. Income tax was temporary 100 years ago, it is due for demise. Also, it is expensive to administer and ineffective.

If you thought that life was harder than it should be, the problem is that you are carrying parasites on your back. It is time to shrug them off.

We are resonating with fundamental ideas embraced by the majority, that good guys should flourish, that the government should serve, that we need to make a society that provides opportunity for everyone, that we need to allow our young people to find their passion and pursue it, that we need to find better ways of placing mothers at the centre of society, that people are entitled to low-cost reliable electricity and all of the other ideas mentioned above.

Reptile Brain

We are not about tickling the brainstem - that you inherited from the dinosaurs - to create hysteria about climate in 30 years time, George Floyd, allegations of rape at universities, gay liason, pronouns, allegations of misogyny, allegations about racism by racists and other nonsense.

We Know How To Live

We all know how to live, we just need the government off our back so that we can get on with our life. The fringe-dwellers should get beyond the fringe and shut up.

We have written this manifesto because currently things are 'going to shit' and it is up to us to turn things around and restore some Aussie delight in life.

Therefore, please apply your own insights and let's get things moving.

I record a few thoughts below in case they are useful.

Story So Far

In the story so far we have given recognition to some of the Plucky Aussies who helped to build Australia, considered some of the events that got us to here, examined some of our institutions and made the case for improvement, identified some of the industries where Australia should lead the world, what remains is to consider how we might enable the glorious future available to Australia.

We Pay The Bills

Already the Productive Aussies pay the bills, not just for themselves, but also for a vast, and growing parasite and passenger class, more than 2 million people. It is not sustainable, there are too many of them and their cost keeps going up and up.

A majority of Aussies know that this is true, that we need to restore respect for the people who make it all work and give them a break.

The Marxist virus has infected too many people, we need to help them to recover from this degrading disease.

Lefty Whispers

The lefties took control in the 1980s, by deliberately populating every committee and decision-making body in the country with their nominees. They then, spent vast amounts of money, damaged our international reputation, doubled the price of electricity, diminished business, forgot to build roads or dams and filled the air with brainless clichés.

It is time to restore some balance.

We need responsible people in positions of power, not closet marxists or sly rent-seeking subversives. The productive people should be much better represented on committees and decision-making bodies across our wide brown land.

We need to build frameworks that allow people to go about their business with minimal abuse by governments. As advocated by Elon Musk, fewer meetings, shorter meetings, focus on what needs to be done, not precious posturing.

Option 1: The Quiet Approach

In this approach, we would not discuss the ZIT Party in the public arena. Talk quietly to Productive Aussies that you trust about the need to get the parasite's thieving hands out of our pockets and the regulators off our backs. Expand the number of people who understand the issue and who will vote for serious candidates.

The majority of Aussies know that we are heading in the wrong direction.

Bypass The Narcissists

The next step is to recruit serious candidates for every office, from school council and municipal council to state and federal politics.   Do not wait for people to nominate themselves, narcissists are not useful, except to themselves.

Explain to your selected candidate, that they will get wide community support, not just for the official role, but also for their business and private life if they wish, including baby-sitting. The best people may be reluctant, explain that we need them to help restore the decency and freedom of Aussies, that this adventure will be short term and very well supported.

My suggestion is that we assure them that they can move on after a few years. People with a good life may not wish to spend extended periods in these public roles. We should share the load, give many people a go. Back them up with extensive support, both in policy formation and implementation.

Plucky Aussies should look after one another and block the abusive, spendthrift parasites.

Independents

Picture multiple candidates with interlocking preferences standing as independents, promising lower taxes in every lower house federal constituency across the country. You will know the local issues that need attention.

These candidates should lead a 'policy forum' in each constituency. This forum should continue after the election to ensure that the elected politician is provided with broad based information on the thinking of the voters.

Once in parliament we can discuss how to work together.

Jill And Jack

What about, in each constituency, two candidates in their twenties, two in their thirties, two in their forties, two in their fifties, and so on, take it as far as you like. Is it too old-fashioned to suggest that there are two genders and that we might have representatives of each standing in every electorate? In this way we get advice and involvement from all age groups and both genders.

The majority of Australians do not support the current clowns and would vote for candidates who would set them free.

Structure

The structure of each branch should be whatever works for you, this is a grassroots movement. However, may I put some thoughts on the table?

What if all positions were shared between the genders, both a Female President and a Male President and so on for secretary, treasurer, recruitment director, events director. Every decade should be represented, in all policy discussions and as candidates. Branches could be any size between 10 and 200.

Some branches might be all millennials, some all retirees, some a melange and every other combination. Different strokes for different folks. Since forever, people have tended to spend time with other people similar to themselves, it works well. Do whatever works for you.

The Result

We will end up with Zero Income Tax, fewer regulations and a good life for the productive people.

Option 2: Take Them On In The Public Square

Publicly declare the ZIT Party and deal directly with the brainless, dirty, personal abuse that will follow from the shriekers. We are not seeking to convert the ABC, Nine newspapers and other party political organisations to democracy. They have disappeared down the rabbit hole and cannot find their way out.

Stand for ZIT Party, promising zero income tax, fewer regulations, improved institutions, world class industries, a discussion about immigration and a prosperous future.

Hollera

Income tax will be cancelled as at the previous July 1. All pre-payments will be refunded. Tell them to 'get stuffed'. 'Fuck Off' is the most useful phrase in English or any other language.
Swear words capture what the culture is afraid of, for the English it is sex, the Northern Europeans have 'Hollera', as in 'cholera upon you'. Italians 'a fanabla', Chinese '妈的', Indian 'behnchod' and so on. Disease-based imprecations may be more appropriate in 2021.
Right now we are in a totalitarian phase where the political police are authorised to bash you. We should be careful and discreet until we get the fascists behind bars.
George H. W. Bush encouraged the Shia Marsh Arabs to stand against Saddam Hussein and then did not support them. Thirty thousand were killed and the marshes that supported their lifestyle were drained.

Make It Right

We have allowed our politics to become perverted. We need to fix it. No longer 'she'll be right', but 'we will make it right'.
It is time.
Let's do it.

PLUCKY AUSSIES

Rum Voyage

Hamilton shouted 'we are sinking'. The yacht hit the sand-bar and stuck, with the decks under water. Greatly relieved to avoid drowning, the crew of 50 scrambled ashore onto a small island in Bass Strait, now called Preservation Island. They had been at sea for months in a leaky boat heading from Calcutta, via Cape Leeuwin, to the South of Tasmania, aiming for the infant colony at Sydney Cove in 1797 with rum and other supplies. The colony was 9 years old and not sustainable, being short of food, rum, skills and discipline.

Hamilton considered his position, the crew were ashore, much of the cargo could be saved, however, there would be no passing ships and the settlement at Sydney Cove was 500 miles away.

He asked Thompson, Clarke and Bennet to take the longboat, sail to Sydney Cove and get help. They sailed across Bass Straight and along the 90 mile beach until a storm drove them ashore. Another shipwreck.

With some saved supplies they headed North on foot through territory never before seen by Europeans, but well understood by the local tribes. Clarke knew nothing about tribal cultures or the territory he was traversing, he was originally from Scotland, more recently a merchant in Calcutta.

Gunaikurnai People

We now know that they were passing through the territory

of the Gunaikurnai People, specifically the Tatungalung family clan. The Gunaikurnai saw the white people as the returned spirits of their ancestors, 'jump up white'. The clan observed, but did not make contact with this bedraggled group heading North through their territory.

Our First Peoples cultures had evolved over tens of thousands of years. Each tribe had elaborate rules that governed conduct both within the tribe and between adjacent tribes. Within the tribe everyone was 'equal', however tribal elders were to be obeyed, women did much of the work and infanticide kept the numbers down so that resources were adequate and the gene pool improving. Between tribes, there was negotiation, display, Corroboree line dancing, some females changing tribes, some battles and some collaboration, for example feasting on the Bogong Moths in the high country or the fish at Lake Mungo, each being plentiful at some times of year. Deep knowledge of local flora and fauna enabled a sound diet and an easy life, two hours of hunting per day was enough.

The shipwreck party had none of this knowledge and had to depend upon some rice salvaged from the wreck.

Rafting

Clarke kept a diary and recorded that walking along the 90 mile beach was easy until they came to a river. They built a raft. It sank. Trying again with dry timber they got across. And, so it was with each river crossing, build the raft, get across, then leave the raft behind and continue the trek North.

Genitalia

On the 4th day, 14 aboriginal men came into view, Clarke records that the locals wished to investigate these strange paleskins. Aboriginal men were naked, so their assumption was that these clothed people with no genitals on display, were female. They opened the shirts of the trekkers, looking for breasts and were both startled and amused to find hairy chests.

Clarke observed that these locals had large heads and seemed fit and strong. They were adorned with bones in their hair and through the nose septum plus rancid fish oil in their hair. This did not appeal to Western sensibilities. The encounter provided insights to both parties. There was no violence and the trekkers continued on their way.

Now, some thoughts on the first fleet.

Bound For Botany Bay

The surgeon on the founding voyage in 1787 was George Worgan, let us make him an honorary Aussie. The information in the next segment comes from his journal of the voyage.

On board were chooks, goats, pigs, sheep, horses, cows and bulls, plus vegetable seeds and fruit trees, some convicts and some soldiers. 'When we arrived in Botany Bay we saw some natives, they were of a black reddish sooty colour, entirely naked, walked very upright, and each of them had long spears and a short stick in their hands'. The aborigines and the new arrivals were unsure of one another, some peaceful gestures by both parties and an exchange of presents enabled some interaction. The locals guided the new arrivals to a source of fresh water.

After checking out an adjacent inlet, the decision was made to abandon Botany Bay and to establish the penal outpost in Port Jackson. On 26 January 1788 the governor and some officers went ashore and made a toast to the success of the colony.

The colony struggled to feed itself and in the early days used rum as both a social lubricant and a currency. Therefore rum was precious and highly valued. This information, percolating to merchants in Calcutta had triggered the voyage of the 'Sydney Cove' to bring supplies.

Travelling North

The shipwreck squad reached Wingan Inlet on day 5, made a raft and floated across the river and kept going to Mallacouta. Another raft, another crossing. Then on to Cape Howe with sand dunes and shell mounds from Aboriginal feasting. These mounds showed that the Aboriginal people harvested seafood and lived well. Meanwhile, the shipwreck party were very short of food.

At Nadgee river they encountered a group of the Thaua Aboriginal people, who accepted some gifts and allowed them to pass. Another opportunity for both parties to learn a little about one another.

Clarke and Bennet had few choices, they were few in number, poorly armed and poorly fed. First they sought to establish that they had not come to fight, arms outstretched empty palms facing forward. Next, they sought to show that they were just passing through, heading North.

There was some shared understanding, the locals showed trekkers the established paths through the woodland, this made the walking much easier, and the shipwreck party continued on.

Thaua Women

The Thaua men allowed their women to be seen - a sign of trust or perhaps an insight the fact that the shipwreck party posed no threat. The Thaua women were greatly amused by these scrappy creatures.

The women had many skills, harvesting yams, preparing grains, fishing, midwifery and infanticide. Then - as now - some of the fighting was over access to women.

Encounters

Later, they reached the river at Wonboyn and set to building a raft. Some of the Aborigines from the day before appeared and helped the Europeans across. In the following days they were shown Aboriginal paths and helped across rivers all the way to Twofold Bay, where the Aboriginals gave them a much needed shellfish meal.

Is it true that the aboriginals collaborated with killer whales to harvest lower order whales, feeding the delicious tongues of the victims the killers?

After crossing Murra River a mob of 50 Aboriginals with spears appeared. Ignoring the threat, Clarke proceeded towards them, exchanged some gifts and was allowed to proceed. The same crowd threatened the trekkers on the following day. Some negotiation with the elders allowed them to continue.

Next day near the Bermagui River the same natives came from behind and appeared hostile. The trekkers readied for battle with one gun, two pistols and some clubs. Perhaps this display earned some respect and conflict was avoided. After some negotiation, a kangaroo tail was exchanged for some cloth and they were allowed to straggle on.

Walbanga Mob

When the trekkers reached Wallaga Lake, they met the Walbanga Mob of the Yuin people and found that this group had a friendly disposition. The trekkers thought that they understood that the Walbanga were at war with the neighbouring Thaua.

The trek continued with further assistance from the locals in finding tracks and crossing rivers. Clarke finally reached Sydney and boats were sent to Bass Strait to rescue Hamilton and the others.

Clarke became a merchant in Sydney.

Sydney Cove Colony

The Sydney Cove colony was supposed to be self-sufficient, however the land close to Sydney was not fertile, the colonists were not farmers and supplies were running short - food, fabric, ropes, axes and more. The planning for the expedition had been both negligent and deficient. No consideration of the local conditions and no thought about the skills needed to found a colony. Just dump the convicts far away. Later fleets included some people with useful skills to help build a workable colony.

The merchant voyage from Calcutta to Sydney Cove demonstrates the courage and initiative of the Scottish who were often found at the edges of - and did the heavy lifting in - the British Empire. There was no order for supplies from Sydney, the British government having given a monopoly of supply to the East India Company. The Scottish merchants in Calcutta heard about the shortages and sent supplies.

This is an excellent example of Adam Smith's, 'Invisible Hand', the creation of a fruitful society by the agglomeration of initiatives by the citizens. Australia has benefitted from the actions of plucky individuals and groups throughout the long Aboriginal evolution and the short history since European settlement.

Let us move forward to the arrival of Lachlan Macquarie as the fifth governor of the colony of New South Wales in 1810.

Macquarie

Lachlan Macquarie came from a subsistence farm on the island of Mull in Scotland, through military service in India to arrive in Sydney as the fifth governor of the colony in 1809. He had been briefed on the 'Rum Rebellion', where the bombastic Governor Bligh had been deposed. This was to some extent a 'poisoned chalice'. His first views of Sydney showed that it was small, undeveloped and suffered from both poverty and disorder.

The parliament in England saw the colony as a remote gaol that should learn to pay its own bills, Macquarie perceived the opportunity to create a new country. His early experience in poverty in Scotland meant that he was sympathetic to the situation of the convicts and he set out to provide a pathway for them to demonstrate that they were ready to resume a normal life with full rights of citizenship.

This approach laid the foundations for the egalitarian society that was to characterise Australia and to some extent persists today.

Firm And Fair

For his part Macquarie set out to uphold high moral standards and to be fair but firm to rich and poor, man and woman, black and white. His vision was for a society where people got along in a civilised manner and where there was opportunity for all. However the traditional family loyalty principle was also in play, in the appointment of members of his own family to roles in Sydney.

He believed that it was possible to have good relations with the aboriginals, that their rights should be protected by law and that they should be treated with kindness.

Getting Organised

Macquarie had absolute authority over a territory which included New Zealand, The Solomon Islands and Fiji, plus the Eastern half of Australia.

In Sydney, he set aside land for the production of wheat and potatoes to feed the population. Curious that this basic food production function was not in place 22 years (1788 - 1810) after the foundation of the settlement. He also instructed that housing should be moved above the floodplain of the Hawkesbury river. More than 200 years later we are still learning this lesson as the recent floods attest.

Meanwhile Elizabeth McArthur was developing the family sheep business South of Sydney.

Elizabeth Macarthur

Elizabeth McArthur was the doyenne of the top social circle in Sydney, bringing both wit and charm to the party. She enjoyed the climate, the produce, the house, the farm and the gracious lifestyle. Meanwhile, her husband John was away in the UK for 10 years, discussing his role in the insurrection that removed Bligh from the Governor's role and also importantly establishing the reputation of and the sale of Australian wool.

In his absence, Elizabeth very successfully managed the improvement of the sheep flock, the estate, and the education of their children.

Back To Macquarie

Macquarie ensured that a hospital, barracks, roads and bridges were built, in total 265 works were carried out during his reign. His pronouncements led to an increase in the rate of marriage, attendance at church and the rehabilitation of convicts and a reduction in the number of public houses.

Macquarie sought to reach out to the First Peoples, commissioning for them a school, village, farm and annual celebration. However the cultural gap was immense and what were seen by the Europeans as 'hostile acts' by the tribal people continued. The communal sharing which was normal in aboriginal communities was seen as 'thieving' by the new arrivals.

It is not surprising that people on the wrong end of dispossession would seek to defend their world.

Trepang

The Yolŋu people of Arnhem Land traded with visitors from Indonesia from 1700, probably earlier. The trade included cloth, axes and knives, enriching Yolŋu life. In the mid 1800s one third of Chinese annual demand for trepang - 900 tons - was supplied from Arnhem Land.

Lieutenant Collins

Lieutenant Collins was sent from England to discover the potential of the Port Philip Region. He turned right upon entering Port Philip Bay and established a trial settlement at Sullivan's Cove in Sorrento. Water was scarce, the land was sandy, the natives hostile and Collins thought that he would have better career opportunities in Hobart.
Some convicts including William Buckley escaped.

Buckley's

William Buckley lived for 32 years with the Wathaurong people and found their food to be better than the slop that had been served on the voyage out. He became a member of the tribe, speaking their language, following their customs, was married and expanded his family with a daughter.
Our First Peoples inhabited cultures that had evolved over tens of thousands of years with detailed social conventions for behaviour both within and between tribes. They were well fed, happy and resilient.
Later Buckley was an interpreter between the tribes and the settlers, but felt that he was not trusted by either side, both of whom adhered to their own cultural perspectives. The English with an empire and gunpowder knew that they were superior and that people not like them were - by definition - savages.
Buckley moved to Tasmania to escape from the intercultural tension.

Convict Architect

Frances Greenaway designed the Supreme Court in Sydney, Saint James Church and much more, prisons, stables, barracks and lighthouses.

Convict Surgeon

William Redfern transported for mutiny, practiced as a surgeon on Norfolk Island and in Sydney and was superintendent of the the Dawes Point Hospital.

Culture Warrior

Bennelong straddled the cultural gap between Aboriginal and European culture. He spent 3 years in London, meeting many people and going to the theatre and museums. On return he chose to live his traditional life, becoming an elder of his tribe and fighting battles.

Stripper

John Ridley in 1843 built a stripper to improve efficiency by mechanically getting the wheat off the stalk. Australians were early adopters of useful ideas especially the production and use of harvesting machines and much later computers.

New And Better America

Charles Duffy in 1856 said, 'we are making a new and better America'. He sponsored a private member's bill to remove property as a qualification for membership of the NSW Assembly.

Archer Family

The Archer family drove some sheep North and established the first farm in what later became Townsville. Then they had a sailing cutter built to bring materials in and take produce out, on the tidal river. No Government approval or assistance needed. Colin was later a celebrated yacht designer in Norway.

Hospital For Women

Diamantina Bowen was 26 when she arrived in Brisbane from the Greek island of Zanthes. Diamantina cared about the welfare of women and girls and led a committee to establish a hospital for women.

Nurses

Lucy Osburn trained nurses in 1868. 'In her time at Sydney hospital she had successfully trained many Nightingale nurses and established the Nightingale focus of cleanliness, sanitation and fresh air and adequate food'.

Ice With That?

James Harrison in 1854, invented the mechanical ice maker. Until then ice had been cut from a lake outside Boston and sent by sailing ship to Australia. The gentlemen of the Melbourne Club claimed to be able to identify by taste the origin of the ice. This invention allowed Australian produce to be refrigerated and sent to Europe, greatly expanding trade opportunities.

Negotiation

Tommy McCrae of the Wahgunyah tribe on the River Murray, in 1880 captured the courage of tribesmen in a series of sketches. One image shows an elder from each clan in a forward position negotiating, while the warriors from each clan were lined up further back. Measured discussion to avoid conflict, with the threat of force if necessary. Sometime later this approach was adopted by Theodore Roosevelt 'speak softly and carry a big stick'.
Early social distancing. Disease spreading cities and extensive

travel not part of tribal life. Larger gatherings happened in summer when diseases were less likely to spread. Covid is helping us to re-learn these lessons.

Mary Penfold

Mary Penfold managed the family winery begun in 1844 until her retirement in 1884 at the age of 68. The original aim was to produce a wine-based health tonic. Now we have Grange Hermitage, one of the finest wines in the world.

The Hiking Politician

Jimmy McLachlan stood up for the little guys in difficult times. He believed that parliament 'should be an instrument to address the wrongs and injustices that appear to be inherent in our social, economic and financial structures'. He knew the names of most of his 11,000 constituents and visited them on foot to understand their situation. The voters kept him in office from 1908 to 1938, demonstrating their appreciation of his efforts.

Albert Namatjira

Albert Namatjira of the Arrernte people was versatile, working as a carpenter, blacksmith and stockman plus making boomerangs and woomeras. He was also a well known painter. One of his works hung on the wall of my 12 person primary school.

Moderate And Conciliatory

William Spence created unions in the mining and pastoral industries and co-ordinated action across Australia. He demonstrated that unity could force employers to improve wages and conditions. As usual the privileged classes did not wish to share increasing prosperity with the workers, creating the need for union action.

Polite And Flash

Joseph Jenkins in 1871 carried his swag as he walked in search of work. He went to the International Exhibition in Melbourne 1881. 'This town is managed as polite and flash as any town in England but little more forward in pride'.

Hugh Mckay

Hugh McKay built a harvester on the farm at Drummartin in Country Victoria and patented it in 1885. This innovation improved the productivity on the farm and grew to become a business that built 500 harvesters in 1901.

The company town at Sunshine included accommodation, electricity, church, tree lined roads, tennis courts and gardens for workers, plus world class equipment in the factory. Who knew, world class manufacturing and a great life for workers, before Federation.

Rust Resistant Wheat

William Farrer bred rust resistant wheat, which helped treble the wheat harvest in Australia. A 'Rust in Wheat' conference was held in 1890 leading to more experimentation and better wheat. Another Aussie first.

High Watermark Of Popular Government

James Bryce was an Englishman who had researched the US constitution. His view of the Australian constitution: 'It represents the high watermark of popular government. It is penetrated by the spirit of democracy'.

Australia launched with both care and confidence.

How did this degrade to house arrest and a gestapo style curfew over a flu virus?

Stump Jump Plough

In the Mallee Region the residual roots of eucalyptus scrub wrecked ploughs. Grubbing out all of the roots was very expensive, so Aussie innovators Richard and Clarence Smith invented the 'Stump-Jump Plough'. This allowed the continued expansion of wheat growing in the Mallee lands.

Earl Page

Earle Page believed that the government action was important in the development of a new nation, infrastructure, industry, mining, land settlement including the Bradfield scheme to divert rivers inland, to liberate the arid interior. The Bradfield ideas are again being considered in 2021. It is about time.

Just Do It

Guy Menzies flew to NZ in 1931. Official plan was a trip to Perth, he just flew to NZ because he felt like it. Crash landed in a swamp … whatever.

World Champion From 1933 To 1950

Walter Lindrum in 1932 made a billiards break of more than 4,000 points, his speciality was 'nursery cannons' - look it up and get some practice.

Aviatrix

Maude Lores Bonney flew around Australia in 1932, then to England and South Africa. She led the Women's International Association of Aeronautics and the Australian Women Pilots' Association.

Paspaley

Nic the Greek Paspaley in 1932 had his own pearling lugger and was harvesting shell for button making. The family business now includes pastoral, commercial, retail and aviation interests. Perhaps we should convene an advisory parliament for Australia, containing Aussies with Greek origins.

Aspro

George Nicholas experimented in the backroom of his pharmacy to discover a pain relief drug and created 'Aspro'. He built innovative factories in UK and Australia and showed the world how to treat staff well and flourish.

Antarctica

Philip Law led many research and mapping voyages to Antarctica. Picture being snowbound for months. Recording and transmitting a wide range of information, atmospheric, scientific, meteorological, mapping, radio transmission, biological, physiological and geophysical to the world.
Philip told me that libations from the barrel of port he kept in his office helped to smooth the inevitable, interpersonal irritations.

Myxo

Rabbits were brought to Australia to provide some amusement to the shooting class. The rabbits liked it here and created a plague that did immense damage across the country.
Ian Clunies Ross studied parasites and later supported the use of myxomatosis to deal with the rabbit plague. He injected himself with myxo to prove that it was not harmful to humans.

Fletcher Jones

David Fletcher Jones started in struggle street, yet built one of the largest clothing companies in the world. He believed that business should contribute to society not just make a profit. Heard that lately?

Margaret River

Tom Cullity got his doctor's ticket at Adelaide University and was at the the first Barossa Vintage Festival. He went to France and Germany seeking wine wisdom. Later he was the first to plant Riesling and Cabernet at Margaret River.

Syme On Protection

In 1851 David Syme tried his hand on the Californian gold fields and later on the Victorian gold fields. A family connection led to him becoming the publisher and editor of 'The Age' from 1860. His key issues were: 'land for the people, protection for native industries, full rights of self-government'. He became a strong supporter of protection.

The Age opposed Speight, 'accusing him of extravagance, incompetence, dereliction of duty, and contempt of parliament and the public'. These issues persist.

Alfred Deakin, on the way to Federation, learned a great deal about both politics and journalism from Syme.

Deakin On Federation

'Instead of being forced into partnership by a crisis, it will be far better for us to be united before the crisis arrives, so that we may face it with a bold and unbroken front.' Self-interested, intransigent Sydney-siders would not join unless the synthetic capital was placed in their state.

Ned Kelly

Ned liberated the valuables from travellers in Central Victoria to support his hard-scrabble farming family. He engaged in a legendary shoot-out with the police wearing home made armour.
His story plays to our hope that the 'little guy' will get a break.
Mick Jagger got some satisfaction playing Ned in the movie.
Police then, as now, abusing the poor to protect the property of the rich.

Forrests

The distant Uncle of Andrew was Premier of Western Australia, explorer, builder of the long water pipe line to Kalgoorlie and developer of Minderoo station.
Andrew is the fourth generation of the Forrests in WA and founder of the Fortescue Metals Group. As a child he fraternised with Pilbara tribal peoples around Minderoo and learnt their language.
He is helping us to think clearly and sympathetically about issues relating to our First Peoples and to understand the potential of Hydrogen as both a source and store of energy. NSW has committed $3 billion to the hydrogen project.

Silly Billy

In the 1950's nuclear testing took place in Australia, we had access to the data. In 1958 we built the first nuclear reactor in the southern hemisphere as a step towards nuclear based electricity. Land was allocated at Jervis Bay for a nuclear power generation plant and steelworks, teners were closed on 15 June 1970.
Kieth Alder was part of the team of 70 fulltime and 150

part time scientists and engineers involved in the project. Our experts evaluated 14 submissions and selected a British offering. Billy McMahon killed the project.

Once more, we were there at the beginning, but through inferior decision making, discarded the opportunities.

Black Box Flight Recorder

David Warren in 1954 invented the black box flight recorder to capture both conversation and data in the cockpit and facilitate the diagnosis of the cause of a crash. Management did not understand the significance of this device, and did not support the project, so Warren put it together at home in his garage. The management failure to secure patents meant that opportunists elsewhere in the world made the money from this innovation.

Once again a Plucky Aussie with initiative, creates the opportunity. We need to become much better at translating these opportunities into world leading industries. Much of our current managerial class is mediocre.

Yellow Tail

Filippo and Maria Casella came from Italy to Australia in 1957 to find a better way of life. They created a winery and did the finest family Sunday lunch. Mission accomplished.

Son John captured 10% of the value end of the US wine market with 'Yellowtail'. Now they are into beer, violating the industry aphorism that 'grain and grape do not mix'.

Brilliant achievements.

Invent The Computer

Trevor Piercy built one of the first 10 computers in the world here in Melbourne Australia. It is still running at the Melbourne Museum. Oh, they built one in Sydney too.

A political decision to divert funding towards rain-making

meant that we did not translate this leadership position into a technology industry. Perhaps this decision is understandable, drought was real and immediate and no one knew how computers would transform our lives.

Nevertheless a missed opportunity.

Elizabeth Couchman

Elizabeth was a highly valued advisor to Robert Menzies, and enabled women's equal participation in the Victorian section of the Liberal Party. Appointed to the ABC in 1932, she visited Canada, New York and London to study approaches to public broadcasting.

Australia's representative in Paris at an International Council of Women, she delivered a speech in French at the Sorbonne.

Uncle Reg

Reg Ansett started life driving a taxi in Maryborough. Blocked by Menzies from competing with the state-owned railways he started an airline which grew to span the nation.

Margaret Guilfoyle

Dame Margaret Guilfoyle brought to the parliament social and financial insight and her views on drug abuse, higher education, Aboriginal health, ASIO, social services, child care, and the two-airline policy.

Enid Lyons

Enid was elected to the Australian Parliament in 1943. She had been active in politics for many years, travelling widely and making many speeches seeking justice, security and equity and on other issues such as the aluminium industry (the act enabling the development of the Bell Bay Aluminium

Smelter was passed in 1944), nuclear energy (Lucas heights opened in 1958) and other matters including immigration and international affairs. She achieved progress in medical treatment for pensioners, distribution of drugs and child endowment.

From 1951 to 1962 she was a commissioner of the ABC, bringing her understanding of the world to the attention of the early chairs Boyer and Darling, helping the ABC to be relevant and useful.

Don Bradman

The Don was a farm boy who practised his batting alone with a cricket stump and a golf ball up against a wall. He had the ability, did the work and was a great champion. Another Aussie delivering a performance that was the best in the world.

Thank you Don for reminding us that ability and performance are admirable.

Blow Your Horn

Barry Tuckwell was a globally known French Horn aficionado. He joined the Melbourne Symphony Orchestra at the age of 15. Another world-class Aussie.

Janet Clarke

Janet was at the centre of Victorian High society for 30 years, hosting garden parties, balls, lunches and dinners. She accepted the responsibility that fortunate people had towards the less fortunate, 'noblesse oblige', supporting, educational, cultural, philanthropic and political activities.

Charles Court

Charles was Premier of Western Australia from 1974 to 1982, superintending the development of the irrigation scheme at Ord River, the commencement of iron ore extraction in the Pilbara, supporting industrial projects in Kwinana, the North West Shelf gas project and the launch of Murdoch University.

Pansy Wright

Pansy was his own man, delivering arresting lectures and actively participating in public debates. Do you remember when 'debates' were a thing.

At a Physiology lecture Pansy had a decapitated dog on the bench with catheters and other instruments installed to monitor the reaction to the injection of various potions. The triggerati and the brainless zealots would not have been pleased. We were delighted to have an interesting lecturer.

Insiders will know the stories about 'in my hand I hold a syphilised penis' and the height of a washbasin. Voice from the back of the class, 'which hand'?

Both a significant researcher and a mentor of other researchers, he went on to be Dean of Medicine, Veterinary Science and Science.

The modern brainless mob would have cancelled him. Are we making progress?

Germs - Strumpet Voluntary

Germaine Greer wrote 'The Female Eunuch" encouraging women to 'get out more'. Germs shared an apartment with some Aussie young ladies in 1960s London, one of whom was seeking to emulate JFK by having a different sexual partner every day, we all have our own personal goals. As December 31 approached, our amoureuse was last seen in urgent discussion with the postman.

Commenting on female involvement in politics in 1972 in the US 'Womanlike, they did not want to get tough with their man, and

so, womanlike, they got screwed'.
Clive James, was a fan writing on 'The Female Eunuch': 'It is without question the most important single thing yet to emerge from our generation of Australian exiles'.
Federico Fellini was also on the list, exchanging 'bon mots' throughout his life.
Margy Burn quotes Germs on women 'I have suffered a great deal at the hands of women, nuns, nurses, sexual rivals, and I had as a result, no interest in their problems at all ... I had made it in a man's world and I reaped the fruits of the rarity of the phenomenon'. 'The time she had spent in developing countries, especially famine-struck Ethiopia, had convinced her that Western Urban Society had lost touch with the most basic and essential human values as practised in other cultures.'

Ben Lexcen

Ben designed the winged keel that won the 1983 America's Cup. Bondy and Bertrand get the publicity, Ben deserves more.

Silver Bodgie

The 'silver bodgie' was Prime Minister from 11 March 1983 to 20 December 1991. A worker from the ACTU offices told me that all the females in the building knew that you should never be in a room with Bob where the door could be closed.
Brittany Higgins would have thrived - no need to go out drinking and dancing till 2AM and then present yourself back in the office on the bosses desk - romance could strike at any time. How attitudes change.
Reputed to be a drunk and a womaniser, Bob managed to resolve many industrial disputes and be an effective Prime Minister. The Accord between unions, bosses and politicians was a major achievement moderating direct wage claims in favour of a 'social wage'.

Hasluck

His values, stressing the importance of family, education and hard work, were those of the pre-war generation before Australia came to regard itself as the 'lucky country'.

Peter Sculthorpe

Peter created 'Sun Music' and many other pieces evocative of place.

Lang Hancock

Hancock at 26 managed the family cattle station, then was into mining asbestos, lead, tin and copper. Later he helped to break the Federal Government prohibition on the export of iron ore. He was an advocate of minimising government interference in society.

Immunology

Gus Nossal was director of the Walter and Eliza Hall Institute, leading research in immunology and encouraging a generation of researchers in parasitology, haematology, neural development and molecular biology.

Comrade Ambassador

Stephen FitzGerald visited China with Gough in 1971. Zhou sought to upstage Kissinger with a prior Australian visit. True believers celebrate the brilliance of Gough. Zhou showed some brilliance as a diplomat.

In 1971 China was using the blocking of wheat sales to press for a change of government in Australia. It worked. Is the current trade fracas an echo of this Chinese pressure?

Not only was Stephen a great ambassador, but also hosted visits by Melbourne University students, singing 'The East is Red' in full throat, at the banquet. Thank you Jan.

Nuclear Power

Kieth Alder was part of the team of 70 fulltime and 150 part time scientists and engineers involved in the project to build a nuclear power station in Jervis Bay. Tenders closed in 15 June 1970. Our experts evaluated 14 submissions and selected a British offering.

Wine Packaging

Thomas Angove invented the goon bag in 1965. Aussie practicality, a cardboard box with a plastic insert to keep the air away from the wine so that it lasts longer. Across the world, people have been benefitting from this innovation ever since.

Aussie Practicality

Boyd Munro developed spooling software in 1969. Computers could not calculate and print at the same time. Boyd made it happen. Aussie practicality. An early Australian software entrepreneur success story.

Magazine Queen

Ita Buttrose abandoned school at the age of 15 to work for the Daily Telegraph. Later as the editor of CLEO magazine she instituted the nude male centrefold, following in the style of Michelangelo's David.
After many significant media roles, now we hope that she may be able get the ABC to abide by its charter.

Who Invented Wifi

We did. Some radio astronomers at the CSIRO invented WiFi.
The foundation was 'Fast Fourier Transforms' and other fancy
mathematics.
In this case we registered the patent and made some money.

Climate Zealotry

Ian Plimer is a real scientist, who writes about climate. If more
people discovered his work, the apocalyptic hysteria might calm
a little. Please discover his story of the teaspoon.
Some more Aussie independent thinking.

He's My Bro

John So, the first directly elected Lord Mayor of Melbourne, a first
generation immigrant who made a difference and demonstrated
the openness of Australian society.

Aluminium Ferries

Kevin Stanley was one of the founders of Austal our world class,
very successful shipbuilder, defence prime contractor, ferry
designer and manufacturer. (300 vessels, 100 operators, 54
countries)
Did I mention that we might focus on industries that use
Aluminium?

More Manufacturing.

Andrew Liveris started in Darwin and went on to be Chairman
and Chief Executive Officer of The Dow Chemical Company.
Andrew promotes the importance of manufacturing.

We can be global gurus in Aluminium, Nuclear, Space and more.

Innovative Geoscientists

Arvi Parbo sponsored and encouraged innovative geoscientists at Western Mining, leading to major discoveries. His interest enabled the projects. From Tallin via Clausthal Mining Academy to Australia. Coalminer to Chairman.
Sometime soon we will give the green light to Olympic Dam.

Gardasil

Ian Frazer collaborated to create Gardasil which significantly reduces the incidence of HPV cancers. Another Aussie breakthrough. Research continues with a new screening test and refined vaccines.

Bread To The Beaches

Ray Mentiplay supplied the Mornington Peninsula with bread. Following daily demand to produce enough hi-tin, rolls and raisin bread. Ray marshalled the students and other irregulars to get the job done through each summer.

Eh?

Graeme Clark led the team at Cochlear that created the 'bionic ear', delivering the gift of hearing. More groundbreaking research by Aussies.

Ulcer Breakthrough

Barry Marshall, from Kalgoorlie to Perth, US and back, did some breakthrough research on peptic ulcers, and found that surgery was not required.
He showed that Helicobacter Pylori bacteria infections caused

peptic ulcers, leading to effective treatment.

Diffusion Of Innovation

Peter Fenwick launched Fenwick Software in 1976, when we were all seeking to understand how computers should be harnessed to help organisations be more effective. He helped many businesses prosper.

Jelena

Docic defeated Hingis at Wimbledon 6-2, 6-0, at the age of 16, then went on to be no. 4 in the world. We should have seen it coming, she was the world junior champion at the age of 15. From Croatia to Serbia, then Australia. Now a coach and commentator.

Lippy

Poppy King "I couldn't find any lipsticks I liked", so she created a lipstick manufacturing and distribution company. The range included 'Find your Prince' with frog green turns to hot pink lipstick.

Gina Reinhart

Gina is the executive chair of the Hancock Group a major Australian mining group, farmer and sponsor of olympic endeavours.

National Agriculture and Related Industries day | 21 November 2021 | Speech by Gina Rinehart included the following about the 300,000 people who work in agriculture, dealing with red tape, obstruction and theft by government plus foolish employment laws and the 'net zero by 2050' death wish:

'Let me say, I admire your common sense, we need much more of it, especially in government, and your sound Aussie values, and your huge contribution every day, rain hail or shine, droughts floods fires, despite many many difficulties, to our country.'

Peter Ridd

Peter imagined that universities in general and JCU in particular may be interested in research and fact seeking. He was wrong. Moron administrators in the thrall of the climate change religion, presumed the right to silence any view that did not support their deliberately biassed research and their hysteria. They conned Obama.

The great barrier reef has flourished for tens of thousands of years through wide climate variations and will not disappear any time soon.

Peter had a technical loss in court, however, university woke zealots, listen up, your reign is over, we will win the next one and allow ideas to flourish in Academe.

If necessary we will create new institutions and cancel yours.

You've Got To Be In It To Win It

Steven Bradbury was the 'last man standing' and got the gold medal. That's life. My mum said 'you've got to be in it to win it'.

Gail Kelly

Gail was CEO of Westpac, applying a focus on people, clients and staff to deliver great results.

Feed The Chooks

When Joh was Premier of Queensland, he liked to 'feed the chooks', as in put a hand-full of grain out for the journalists to peck at. The journalists for their part engaged in persistent campaign of character assassination, which is still running.

Biased search engines support this smear by returning only negative opinions on Joh. Access to information must improve.

Do these party political hacks masquerading as journalists report that hundreds of Victorians were sent by their preferred party to illegitimately vote in Queensland, thereby corrupting democracy and changing the outcome of an election? 'Whatever it takes'.

However, he was Premier of Queensland from 1968 till 1987, not bad for a guy who left school at the age of 14, had polio which left him with a lifelong limp, and worked on the family dairy farm for 27 years.

As a farmer he pioneered new land clearance techniques and aerial crop spraying and seeding. He was unencumbered by the narrow-mindedness and conformity induced by excessive schooling.

He was elected to state parliament in 1947 at the age of 36 and held this seat for the next 40 years. He is accused of benefitting from a gerrymander. One might ask, to what extent city dwellers generate the prosperity we all enjoy. Perhaps country voters are entitled to greater influence, as they pay for the party we all enjoy.

Queensland flourished under his tutelage, he built dams, electrified the railway system, built power stations, coal mines, airports, bridges, universities, conducted the World Expo in 1988 and the 1982 Commonwealth Games.

Dare one hope that the 'group think' journalistic smear might diminish in due course and a greater appreciation for the contribution Joh made to Australia and Queensland, might emerge.

Courage And Creativity

It was the 'steak and wine' night at the Ballarat Club in 1976, my host Brian Hassett was a progressive General Practitioner who was leading the introduction of computers into medical practices. The speaker was a 28 year old who had been sent from

France to establish a footprint for the the family wine business in Australia. Dominique Portet came from a wine family who already had wineries in France and the Napa Valley and they wished to be established on another continent. Grand strategy indeed.

Dominique had done vintages at Médoc, Rhône Valley, Provence, Moët et Chandon and the Napa Valley, so he was ready to launch in Australia.

"I found fragrance and structure – most of all the structure reminds me of Bordeaux. The Yarra has a charm, a beauty that engulfs you. The wines are worldly."

Since 1976 he has been a pioneer of the renaissance of Australia's cool-climate wine industry, founding renowned sparkling wine house Taltarni in the Pyrenees and Clover Hill in Tasmania.

In 2000 he embarked on his greatest adventure: the Dominique Portet Winery in the Yarra Valley. Check it out.

Troop Transport

In Iraq American troops were sent into battle in Hummers unprotected from roadside bombs, many died. The soldiers welded any iron they could find to the underside of the vehicle, seeking to survive.

Aussies at Thales designed and built the innovative 'Bushmaster' armoured troop transport vehicle, with steel shape to deflect the blast and a water tank to absorb shrapnel that got through. There are more than 1,000 in operation.

'Could A Been' Prime Minister

Mark Latham is now providing insights into Aussie culture to help the infantile, woke, ignorant, yappy class to grow beyond their fantasy bubble of political correctness to see how the world works.

Jolly Swagman

Joe Walker brings the finest interviewees to his podcast, providing extensive insights into economics, politics and life. His deep research and extensive knowledge bring delight to both the audience and the interviewees.

Rna Messages

Peter Waterhouse messes with RNA messaging and has recently discovered how to block transmission. Imagine if you could block the Covid progression. This could be the mouse that roared.

Rupert Murdoch

From managing two Adelaide papers at the age of 23, to the greatest media magnate the world has ever seen, Rupert lived the life portrayed in Rudyard Kipling's 'If' … 'If you can make one heap of all your winnings, and risk it on one turn of pitch-and-toss'.

Rupert was smart, courageous and focussed, the editor of any of 200 newspapers around the world could expect a call from Rupert to discuss the details of the front page of the next edition, managers could expect an informed, detailed discussion of the cost of newsprint paper or any other matter.

Newspapers should capture attention, Col Allan a Rupert acolyte took a sober statistical fact that the number of births outside marriage was increasing and turned this bland fact into an arresting headline 'Nation of Bastards'.

Rudd became Prime Minister because Chris Mitchell - an old Queensland friend of Rudd - persuaded Rupert to back him, yet Rudd is still complaining.

Tony Blair schmoozed Rupert, even making him the godfather of one of his children. Wendy complicated this relationship.

Rupert dodged the 1990s tech misadventures, then later engaged fully with a multi-day briefing and discussion for the top 300 executives at News Limited on how to prosper in an online world.

Rupert has demonstrated that Plucky Aussies can lead the world. We need to apply this insight in more industries.

Millions More

There are millions more Plucky Aussies who have played their part in building this great country. We would like to recognise and celebrate them all.

The next section considers how we 'got to here' through the prism of events.

STILL THEY COME

Populating Australia

Immigrants have had a vast impact on Australia, starting tens of thousands of years ago with our First Peoples, more recently with the 1788 Next Peoples, some boat peoples, some legitimate migrants, plus some rabbits, foxes, sparrows and cane toads producing the current mélange .

There is much more to Australian history than the migrations outlined below and it is well documented elsewhere, from Fatal Shore, to Black Kettle Full Moon, Lucky Country, Lucky Culture, From the Edge, Farmers or Hunter-Gatherers, David Kemp's series starting with 'The Land of Dreams', The Rabbit Proof Fence and many more.

However, for now, let us have a look at some migrations.

Continental Migration

Our first migration, Gondwana to Terra Australis, lush rainforest in a supercontinent at the bottom of the world to the Australian location of today with some of the ferns lingering (Tara Bunga National Park). We are still moving north at 3cm. per year.

Australia and India separated from Antarctica, India went north crashing into the Eurasian land mass and pushing up the Himalayas. Australia over many years of isolation developed the kangaroo, emu, platypus, echidna and many species of snakes, spiders, ants and the salty.

By chance this large lump of rock contained vast mineral

resources, arrived in a location with temperate climate and was waiting for the next migration.

They Are Trying To Kill Me

What did I do wrong? Do these old men really expect me to grovel to them? They are lined up with spears and I am a solitary teenager in front of them. They start throwing spears. The spears fall to one side. More spears are thrown and they are getting closer. What is happening here? These are the elders of my tribe. Why do they wish to do me harm?

By way of context, the convention was that a recalcitrant teenager who wished to reconnect with the tribe would engineer a superficial arm or leg injury to signal a desire for reconciliation. Keep dodging the spears, you will be killed.

Does this remind you of the European duel? A process to eliminate tension within the group.

The next spear came straight at me. I dodged it. They are trying to kill me. I turned and ran, and ran, and ran. I took the raft and paddled and paddled through the night. Around midday the next day I landed on an island. It seemed to be a very big island. Is this the first instance of the Aussie disrespect for authority and the triumph of individuality over group identity?

Yearning To Be Free

Our teenager and whomsoever followed were the first Australians. They had escaped from the tribal rules and had sought freedom. Many generations of immigrants to Australia have come here yearning to be free. They are still coming.

The above account is fictional, there are no records of the first arrival of homo sapiens in Australia, were they refugees or explorers? Did they come by island-hopping or walk across from Papua New Guinea? We do not know.

Deep End Of The Gene Pool

We do know that they were fewer than 100 - with perhaps as few as 5 women with the task of populating a continent. Showing greater insight than European Royalty - haemophilia anyone - they used infanticide to avoid the problems of in-breeding and Mendelian decline, thus moving to the deeper end of the gene pool.

We are currently moving in the opposite direction, imagining that we are superior because we keep every DNA miscue alive. We indulge ourselves with a feel good, short term approach, our First Peoples had a valid (resilient, sustainable) strategy that lasted for tens of thousands of years. In the case of twins, one was killed. When moving camp, the mother had to carry her offspring and other stuff, one child was enough.

Spreading Out

Rising seas separated mainland Australia from New Guinea and Tasmania around 10,000 years ago. Early clans migrated along the coast in both directions, finally meeting on the Nullabor Plain. Imagine that meeting. You have been moving into unoccupied territory for generations and suddenly you see people coming in the opposite direction. Was this a convivial meeting?

Our First Peoples lived a culturally rich, refined and satisfying life. Frestick farming was a much better approach to land management than the current fatal, green-sposored firestorms. Greens causing more deaths, we need to hold them accountable. Scott in 'Against The Grain', tells us that many tribal peoples had a good life and chose not to settle down in agricultural societies with poor diet, no freedom and a megalomaniac strutting about. Then came the convicts.

Convict Chains

In 1788 the First Peoples in Australia were well fed, secure in their identity, living in harmony with nature, with a rich cultural life and intricate rules that that governed relations within and between tribes. 'From each according to ability, to each according to needs', Karl's mantra had been operating effectively in tribes and villages across the world including Australia for millennia.

The First Peoples in Australia had spent tens of thousands of years refining these cultural conventions to high levels of sophistication and efficacy.

The new arrivals were the weird ones, members of a failed culture that could not produce civilised behaviour among its members - millions murdered by psychopaths - and who thought that it was OK to sell minor criminals into slavery on the other side of the world.

Pomposity

The British Industrial Revolution had some merit, however, the treatment of the working people in Britain at the time of the Industrial Revolution was abominable. Monsters in top hat and tails with a gin and tonic in one hand and a whip in the other, casually preying upon any woman in the vicinity. Their culture is still inferior (Rotherham, Rochdale), however their pomposity continues unrivalled.

Enlighten The Enlightenment

The gang of enlightenment thinkers spend a great deal of time talking about individuality. Most people derive their identity, pleasure and satisfaction from participation in like-minded groups. The enlightenment exposition needs to be updated to accommodate the influence of groups on life and society.

Guns, Germs And Steel

The culture inhabited by the members of the first fleet was English Aristocratic Arrogance (rule by brutal clique), leavened by a dash of the recent Native American/Scottish Enlightenment (rationality, individuality) - less refined, less sophisticated and less sustainable than the First Peoples cultures in Australia which had evolved over thousands of years.

However the new arrivals had the guns and violence prevailed.

'Prenez Un Grip'

We might help the British 'get a grip' by posthumously court-marshalling the genocidal generals who sacrificed thousands of volunteer Australians, in two world wars, for negligible gain. These are the pathetic people who handed Singapore to a small, starving, ill-equipped Japanese force invading on bicycles.

Does the recent nuclear submarine deal, AUKUS mean that the genocidal Brits are once again wanting to put Aussies in the forward trenches? They have done this in three out of three wars already. Do you trust our politicians to manage this relationship?

Guns Vs. Spears

A tribal culture that was validated by tens of thousands of years of evolution contrasted with a recent enlightenment experiment that had created factories with child labour and inhumane working conditions, filthy, unhygienic cities and dirty, diseased citizens, governed by a small tribal band of amoral kleptocrats.

Ten year old children, because they were smaller were used to get the lint out of the air ducts, they died of lung complications and did not make adulthood. No problem.

London had such a high death rate that it depended on people coming in from the countryside to maintain its numbers. However, they did bring modern technology, trade, hierarchy, disease, guns and rum.

Push Motivation

The members of the first fleet were a mixed bag, some convicts, some soldiers, some administrators, an odd assortment without the skills required to found a colony. The English just wished to dump their convicts somewhere and did not care about the details. The 'Botany Bay' prison was on the brink of failure for many years.

It was push motivation, the British aristocratic class had been transporting 'convicts' to America and selling them into slavery, that was now blocked and they wanted another remote location in which to dump their desperate underclasses.

This is moral failure on a spectacular scale, have these mafiosi with affected manners received the opprobrium they deserve?

Many 'migrants' to America from Scotland and Ireland, were driven out by a poor harvest or a greedy land owner - sheep more profitable than people. They went as indentured servants, in return for the fare, that is, they signed up as slaves for four or five years.

Monsters

Much of the behaviour of the privileged classes could be construed as theft or murder, perhaps they should have been imprisoned, deported or guillotined.

Did anyone consider providing employment for these citizens, rather than starving and abusing them? Yet the British promoted themselves then and now as a superior race. It is time to re-evaluate these monsters.

Bertrand Russell observed that the problem with power is that it often goes to the people who want it most (eg. Temporarily Dom, then Boris or is it Carrie, perhaps Dylan or locally, Rudd, Gillard, Malcolm, Scomo), these may not be the people who will exercise the power most wisely.

Bastardry

Back to the bastardry, anyone who would not be a slave to the privileged classes was classified as a criminal and exiled. There were 220 offences that led to hanging. Crimes could be as small as stealing a rabbit or a piece of cloth, or any statement that did not support the politics and privileges of those in power.

Gin And Prostitution

This failed English culture which did not provide a survive-able life for many people, created the need to steal to feed your family. A very fancy lifestyle for the few and a desperate struggle for the masses. It focussed on exploitation, rather than job creation and firmly crushed any opposition.

Prostitution and private gin stills were rife, anything to get by.

The rotting hulks in the Thames were overloaded with English citizens re-labelled as criminals. America being no longer available, the decision was taken to dump this policy-created desperate underclass in Botany Bay.

One Out Of Three Aint Bad

There was no plan to colonise the whole country. Very little was known about Australia. However, if the Brits did not grab it, the French, the Dutch or the Germans might. There were tall pines on Norfolk Island that it was believed would be good for masts of ships. Masts were as strategically important as oil became in later years. It was also believed that the convict colony would become self supporting and not be a 'burden on the crown'. So the 'First Fleet' was despatched.

Two of these assumptions were incorrect, Norfolk pines were no good for masts and the colony took many years to become self supporting. The fear of French colonisation was well founded.

French Connection

Joseph Banks may have encouraged the French interest in Australia by sending a platypus to Napoleon. Several French scientific expeditions were despatched. There was a French claim of sovereignty to the Western half of Australia. Fortunately, their research was cut short when they sailed to Polynesia seeking romance.

The British claim to sovereignty was expressed by establishing a footprint at Port Essington in Arnhem Land and putting a cannon on the headland in places like Albany. It was effective.

Ticket Of Leave

The British government wanted their 'criminals' to be severely punished, however Governor Macquarie instead created a ladder of opportunity for convicts leading to the resumption of a place in normal society. This process turned a cynical, ill-considered, badly planned, expedient, remote prison experiment into a country. It also illustrates Aussie (Scottish) independent thinking and a willingness to make a better life for everyone.

George Crossley was transported for perjury in 1799, pardoned in 1801 and went on to own land, run businesses and be a lawyer. There were many other transportees, from architects to surgeons, stonemasons, carpenters, blacksmiths, farmers discarded by Britain who helped to create Australia.

Australia provided the opportunity that England should have offered to its citizens. Classified as a criminal in London, most became reliable citizens in Australia.

An Even Break

Convicts in employment could save money and become property owners, many encouraged their friends and relatives to come to Australia - the land of opportunity. Criminals in London, citizens in Australia - all they needed was an even break.

Convicts supplied the labour to build many of the major civic buildings in early Sydney and enabled the development of many roads and farms. Reliable behaviour led to a 'ticket of leave', a conditional pardon on the way to rehabilitation as a citizen.

The officers of the New South Wales Corps arrived with the convicts, some of them were granted land holdings.

Then came the free settlers.

Settler Migration

The word got around that there was land to be had in Australia, and free settlers began arriving in Sydney Cove in 1793. From 1831 to 1850, 170,000 settlers arrived, with many paying their own fare. There were carpenters, blacksmiths and a sprinkling of lawyers, doctors and priests.

In the 1880s we had the world's highest standard of living and more freedom than any of Henrich's WEIRD societies (Western, Educated, Industrialised, Rich, Democratic).

Resilient Women

Caroline Chisholm in 1836 saw that there were too many single males, leading to arriving single girls being harassed. In the hope of creating a more civilised society she arranged for free passage for the wives and children of emancipated convicts and for the protection of single women. Note that this initiative to create a better society came from Australia, not from England.

Being a mum in early Australia meant that you were the creator of a family, manager of a household, nurse, teacher, chef, clothing manufacturer, counsellor, nutritionist and social convenor. Many young women were employed in domestic service, some were tutors or governesses and some were sharing the work required to develop a new farm, living in small, rough two room 'wattle and daub' houses.

These were resilient women who knew how to make a life without whingeing to the government about every little bump in the road. There are still some around, despite government attempts to buy their vote with promises of a languorous, 'safe' nirvana.

Landed Here Without A Shilling

John Stephens in 1847 sang the praises of South Australia and encouraged Brits to emigrate: 'Many men who landed here without a shilling, and that, too, but a very few years ago, are, at the moment I write, happily settled on their own farms, and surrounded with plenty'.

Fewer convicts, more settlers, stronger families and Australia was on its way.

Gold Migration

The news that gold was lying on the ground, waiting to transform the life of the prospector ricocheted around the world. Gold valued at millions of pounds was discovered in New South Wales and Victoria even before the international gold seekers arrived.

At the time of the gold rushes there was extensive civil strife in China and many sought to escape to Australia, Canada and America. The fear in these destination countries was that their region would be overrun by people from a very different culture. All three countries passed laws to restrict the volume of this migration. Please ignore the contemporary racists who shout 'racism' at everything that is not according to their misunderstanding of history and their political preferences.

Brave, Bold, Hopeful

The brave, the bold and the hopeful came in large numbers during the 1850s, the population of Australia doubling in ten years. The crew of ships arriving in Melbourne jumped ship and headed inland to try their hand on the goldfields. The population of Victoria doubled in one year, 1852.

Shiploads of Chinese arrived in Melbourne during the gold rush. They found accommodation in Little Bourke Street and made their way to the goldfields. They were escaping turmoil in China and hoping for a lucky strike.

People who had experienced democracy in the United States, France, Germany or Italy were among those who came to dig and scrabble at the goldfields. These individuals with both courage and optimism, influenced the discussion on the way to creating Australia at Federation in 1901.

Eureka Lessons

The Eureka uprising was triggered by foolish and unreasonable government policies and heavy handed policing. Did we learn from this feedback? Actually, no. We killed the protesters.

The apparatchiks have not learnt the lesson, that productive people do not wish to be plundered by parasites. Recent fascist-sponsored police attacks on citizens are evidence that we are heading in the wrong direction. Have you seen any recent foolish policy followed by heavy-handed policing?

Charter Of Liberty

Modern Australia was created as the most egalitarian society the European-oriented world had ever seen. Alfred Deakin referred to the constitution as a 'charter of liberty' providing a framework within which Australians might pursue their dreams.

Gold Rush Victoria, splashed its wealth on railways and public buildings. Melbourne was one of the most progressive cities in the world with a grand International Exhibition in 1880. As the gold ran out, the challenge was to provide jobs for the miners and grow the state. Many secured an allotment and went farming.

Saddler In Taradale

My family started with a saddler in Taradale keeping the coaches running during the gold-rush years. When the rail link to Bendigo came through, they loaded up the cart, headed to Sale, established a saddlery business and went into journalism and politics. No begging to the government, that is much more recent.

Migration continued with a flood after the second world war.

European Migration

From 1951 to 1965, 900,000 assisted migrants entered Australia. The population increased by 4 million between 1947 and 1966, evenly split between baby boomer children and immigrants. After Athens, the city with the largest population of Greek origin is Melbourne. After Santiago, the city with the most people from Chile is again Melbourne.

Conviction Politicians

Arthur Calwell as minister for immigration in 1945 'Australia wants, and will welcome, new healthy citizens who are determined to become good Australians'. Arthur spoke his mind and suffered for it. We say that we want conviction politicians, then destroy them.

Arthur at a cricket dinner at the Melbourne Cricket Club reported that he was a few hundred votes short in 1961: 'if the people in this room had voted for me, I would have been Prime

Minister'.

First Strike Nuclear Target

Many came from Eastern Europe to escape from soviet domination, some thought that Australia would be a safe place in the event of a nuclear war. In fact Australia was a first strike nuclear target throughout the cold war as we housed critical military and surveillance assets.
We have benefitted from this migration of Italians, Greeks, Jugslavs, Eastern Europeans, Scandinavians and many more.
Later came the 'boat people'.

Boat People Migration

In 1976, 1989 and 1999 large numbers of economic migrants who desired to grasp for themselves the benefits of living in the open and prosperous society of Australia arrived. Many flew to Indonesia or Malaysia, then paid $30,000 dollars for a shortish ride in a leaky boat towards Australia. Why should these self-selected 'queue jumpers' get priority over legitimate migrants?
Some virtue-signallers pleasure themselves by feigning sympathy for these pretend-refugees. A real refugee is someone who crosses a border in fear of their life. How do you run in fear across the border to Australia? You cannot. None of these people were refugees.
The treaty which they claimed legitimised their 'gate-crashing' behaviour was created after World War II (1951) to allow migration of people across borders within Europe. It has no relevance in 2021 Australia. We should immediately withdraw from this treaty.

Mysterious Policy Perversions

Immigration policy is a mystery. Who decided that in a year when 100,000 immigrants arrived from China, France should be limited to a few thousand and Chile a much smaller number? We need some sunlight to illuminate the policy makers and the policies, so that we can fashion an immigration policy that will support Australia's future.

Finest People In The World

To be allowed to come to live in Australia is a great privilege. No aspirant immigrant has the right of access. Much of the litigation is based upon an assertion of 'refugee rights', firstly they are not refugees, secondly the treaty is not appropriate for Australia in the 21st century. These rights do not exist.

We can select the finest people in the world to come and live here. We have no obligation to accept illiterate, ignorant, lazy or criminal persons, irregardless of whatever back story they can concoct or the scale of the people smuggler fee. We already have too many citizens who do not 'pull their weight'. Zealots of any stripe are not welcome.

Those with skills and culture compatible with Australia should apply in the normal way and will be welcomed. We must make sure that our officials do not put road blocks in front of desirable immigrants, for example South African farmers. Better yet we should encourage immigration by useful people.

Please understand that you will have to do military service and fight for Australia if required. Not prepared to stand up for your new country ... stay away.

Serious Swiss

Serious countries are careful in their immigration decisions. In Switzerland the canton where the immigrants are to be settled must vote in favour of each immigrant. In Japan you cannot apply for a passport till you have lived there for 15 years, and even then your chances of getting in are very limited.

Perhaps we should consider creating a provisional passport, with no voting rights and no right to stand for parliament. This would have blocked both Tony Abbott and Julia Gillard, pleasing two very different sets of people.

If you live a useful life and stay out of trouble, your children can become citizens of Australia. First immigrants should earn their place in Australia. Too many recent arrivals seem to imagine that they have a right to dictate how we live and what we can say.

Hazaras

Some of the boat people were Hazaras from Afghanistan. They were coached in the rules, throw away your passport, claim that you will be killed if you return to your country of origin and appeal the decision if you are not granted entry immediately. The Hazaras have some Iranian ancestry and were being persecuted in the Pashtun regions of Afghanistan. Perhaps they should have headed to Iran. It is, after all, across the border where one can claim to be a legitimate refugee.

Leave Your Troubles Behind

Some recent arrivals seek to involve Australia in the conflicts they ran away from. This is not acceptable. If you wish to be involved in the tension in your country of origin, why did you come here? Go home. Do not seek to waste Australian blood and treasure on the problems you ran away from. I repeat if you care so much - go home.

If you want to deserve your place in Australia, get on with making a life here. Do not bring the hassles from inferior cultures to Australia. Oh ... your home culture is not inferior ... that is another reason for you to go home.

We have built an open culture with opportunity for all. You can be welcome if understand the idea and can contribute to our future.

It is up to you.

Asian Migration

We have Australian citizens of Chinese and Afghan origin who have been here for 5 generations or more. Central Australia was opened up by 2,000 cameleers of Afghan origin. In 1854 in Ballarat ChinTum Lok ran a restaurant serving roast beef and other English-style delights. In the same year there were Chinese lodging houses, merchants, restaurants and provision stores in Little Bourke Street. In 1890 one out of three cooks in Australia were of Chinese origin. By 1970 in Melbourne there were 150 Chinese restaurants. We have been celebrating the Chinese New Year in Little Bourke Street for 160 years.

Racist Bureaucrats

In recent years points gained in the education system have enabled large number of immigrants from China and India. Was this policy? Did some bureaucrat in Canberra decide that we needed more migration from China and India. If so, please raise your hand and explain to us why this was good policy. Was this a racist decision by the bureaucrats, French limited to a few thousand, Chinese 100,000 no problem. For the moron bureaucrats, decisions based on race are racist.

There are at least tens of thousands, perhaps millions of young Europeans who would like to live in Australia. Are they being blocked by another bureaucrat, or is it the same one? Again, please raise your hand and explain your policy. Another bureaucrat is blocking the migration of persecuted farmers from South Africa.

This is our country, we have a right to know who is making this policy and why - whomsoever you are - you think that the current approach is best for Australia. We will facilitate the public discussion of this issue.

Then we panicked over Covid.

Covid Migration

People are leaving the virus-spreading big cities to find smaller communities with less public transport, fewer large shared-air buildings and no maxi-spreader lifts (October 2021). Get out in the open, let the children run, perhaps 'rave culture' meets the family. Others are simply heading North to get away from the Gestapo in Victoria. November 2021 news in Melbourne, we cannot find people to work in hospitality.
Some of the major cities that have disappeared for no apparent reason may have been wiped out by viruses.

Good reason to get out of town.

Poxy Precincts

Life has not, repeat not, been the much publicised 'onwards and upwards' evolution from primitive to civilised. This is a fantasy story created by Europeans to install themselves at the pinnacle of evolution. Perhaps created by courtiers to flatter their masters. You may be aware that courtiers are the most dangerous people, because they separate the decision makers from reality. Think Fauci and Birx misrepresenting the Covid situation.
Dirty, sickly, hungry cities, with a megalomaniac in charge, were not attractive to many. The move from egalitarian hunter gatherer societies to hierarchical, exploitative, narrow diet, violence-based societies is fine for the elite, not so good for the majority.
Latest research suggests that this move to settle was not some sudden pre-ordained transition to a better, more European life, but 3,000 years of experimentation, transitioning to and fro according to the seasons, expediency and personal preference. We have now realised that the hunter gatherers lived a well nourished, healthy, free and happy life and were reluctant to

move to a slave role in a disease-ridden city.

90 Million Person Holocaust

Early American immigrants actively contributed to the holocaust that killed 9 out of 10 native Americans, perhaps 90 million people, in part by distributing disease-infected blankets as gifts. Is this very different from engineering a bat virus with Fauci's 'gain-of-function', to be more transmissible from person to person and then releasing it on the world?

As mentioned above, tribal scale societies have been successfully dealing with diseases for hundreds of thousands of years. The survivors of our species may be the ones who retreat to the tribal scale of society. It is abundantly clear that the policy people are incompetent and cannot save us.

Compulsory jab with an experimental potion that does not prevent death, may even cause death, does not provide immunity, does not prevent transmission and only lasts a few months. An interesting study in the use of fear and terror to manipulate the gullible. Much to be learnt here.

No wonder people are moving to the provinces, seeking to re-discover the village and get some clean air.

Debate On Migration Policy

Australian migration decisions and accidents have had and will continue to have an immense influence on our life, perhaps there could be a public debate to formulate an agreed policy, rather than allowing the continuance of sly, unexplained, secretive decisions by our prandial public servants.

What should our immigration policy be? Have you been engaged in a discussion on this very important subject? Is it on the news? Is it discussed in Parliament? It is time that we explored this issue. Many of the finest people in the world would like to come here, we should welcome them.

Anyone who gets to live in Australia has won first prize in the lottery of life. That includes all of the people who are already here. It is not surprising that many more people wish to come. However, we should not be a dumping ground for detritus. Surprisingly, some morons campaign for Australian to be a garbage collection dump.

Pension Ponzi

Treasury wants to run a Ponzi scheme with new migrants from anywhere expanding the economy to help pay for the ageing population and their extravagant public service pensions. These migrants get older and then we need more migrants. This is how a Ponzi scheme works, you need more deposits to pay the interest to existing customers.
Pauline has 'belled the cat' on this sly Treasury scheme. She directs the big brains at treasury to review the Norwegian experience. If these cosseted, blinkered, irresponsible treasury apparatchiks were of professional calibre, they would have done that already. Is the in-breeding in Canberra decreasing the IQ?

Media - Accessories To Rape

Can we look forward to a public discussion of immigration policy? Perhaps we will continue the 'Rotherham style' failure to address serious issues. The police are already inhibited by a fear of being called 'racist' by the racist chanters in the media both social and what is the other called? Is it downstream media, with a brainless spray of second hand clichés and government and corporate press releases. The media should be held accountable for the failure of police do their job.

Downstream Media

Many jerky journalists (dried out, chewy and stringy) seem to think that they are zealots writing for the Nation Review, a 1960s rag with the single purpose of bringing down the conservative government. Michelle, did you write for the Nation Review?

Perhaps they are just parroting government press releases. One tiny example, the parrots use the term 'fully vaccinated' in the same piece where they are pronouncing the need for a third jab. Clearly, both their brains and their integrity are cactus.

Notice that the editor of 'The Age' Gay Alcorn, regards herself as the publicity arm of the Labor Party, follows the party line and has sacked cartoonist Leunig for behaving like a cartoonist. If she wants to be in politics, she should stand for office. Perverting a once great paper with government propaganda is pathetic. Suggest that you do not waste your money on 'The Age'.

Police - Accessories To Rape

The frequent gang rape of young white girls in Western Sydney by a known cohort of recent immigrants was ignored by both the police and the media. Surely there are people who think that any rape is unacceptable, how then do we allow a pattern of rapes by known groups in Western Sydney? Are the police and the media complicit in these crimes? Can a legal case be made against the media and the police for their complicity in these rapes?

Do these rapists have mothers, sisters, cousins? What do these women think? How would the rapist like their female relatives to be treated?

Should we prohibit migration from their country of origin?

What is life like for a young white female in Western Sydney? You know that the gang can rape you whenever they wish and that no one will do anything about it.

Should young women be able to walk home in safety?

Annoint The Bosses Desk

Brittany Higgins on the other hand chose not to go home,

went out drinking and carousing, then back to the bosses office and onto the desk, she clearly needs better advice on choosing a companion, signalling her desires, selecting locations and a hobby, maybe 'stamp collecting', something beyond 'notching'. Was the photocopier broken?

We need to address these important issues, not just wallow in one celebrity case of 'buyers remorse'.

Explain Yourself

Back to immigration policy. How about we get the sly, dissembling, prandial public servants out into the light of day to explain their closet immigration policy. Better still, we might vote in some politicians who will engage in discussion with the Australian populace to formulate a better immigration policy.

Surveys suggest that Aussies would prefer lower levels of immigration. Are the pollies listening to their voters? No. Surely they are not listening to the ideological incantations of some supposedly trans-national repository of - is it wisdom - or is it wishful thinking? UN chain my heart.

Let us have an Australian debate about who should be eligible, how many is appropriate and what spread of source countries is desirable. Who decided that half of the immigrants should come from one country?

Then we need to consider how to build the infrastructure required. Have the zealots who feel good indulging themselves in virtue-signalling about more immigration made provision for the required infrastructure? Would they like to pay for it? We should help these virtue-signallers understand the cost of their fabulations and grow up.

Earn Your Place

What about a staged process. First, demonstrate that you deserve Australian citizenship. Perhaps a two year visa, extensible by three years and eventually convertible into a provisional citizenship. Earn your place. Then if all goes well, your children can become citizens.

Many immigrants worked on the Snowy Mountains Hydroelectric scheme. We should be grateful for this contribution. Have recent immigrants made a similar contribution?

Rights Of Non Citizens

Too many have scammed the refugee process and are now on unemployment benefits. Perhaps we have to accept these illegitimates who are already here and invite them to become productive Aussies. However, we should not allow any more parasites to sneak in.

How about a moratorium while we build the needed infrastructure, help the new arrivals to become useful members of society, perhaps even help them to learn to speak English. Don't want to speak English, then why did you come here? Suggest that you go to a country that speaks your preferred language.

Malcolm's Goat Herders

Getting an Australian passport is the first prize. We should not casually hand this privilege out to gate-crashers. We can choose. We should choose. We have enough illiterate goat-herders from the mountains. What about some scientists and engineers who can help us to lead the world.

Chart Our Future

Let us have the policy debate and chart our future.
Next, we will examine how our institutions are doing.

CALL TO ACTION

Renaissance

This is the re-birth of Australia.

We started well at Federation. Because our institutions have been perverted, we must now find a way to bring back serious people into the discussion. Instead of debating how many genders, we should be developing industries and improving institutions as discussed above.

It is my belief that these ideas are widely understood.

If you find the ideas expressed here to be a challenge for you, then you are part of the problem. Please try as hard as you can to allow these ideas a place in your understanding of the world. The Marxist fantasies have been tried and exposed as unworkable, many times in many parts of the world.

If you really want to live in a Marxist world, go to a country that follows these ideas. You are not entitled to the prosperity and freedom of Australia, when you actively seek to subvert both the prosperity and the freedom. Does this seem a tad obvious? If you believe that you are entitled to live here while undermining our way of life, then you are a moron. Piss off.

We have had enough abuse and exploitation. We pay the bills and we will call the tune.

We know that the government is the problem, not the answer, freeing our citizens to get on with life rather than being on their knees with a begging bowl to some puffed up, illegitimate, time-serving, self-important 'official'.

We are dancing in the 'circus of life', we have choices, we can make it better or worse. We need 'a bias for action' as recommended by Peters and Waterman.

Policy Choices

A couple of thoughts to illustrate that new approaches are available. It is possible formulate policies that do not need an army of public servants to implement, for example:

On your 18th birthday you receive the details of a company registered in your name, to use or not as you wish.

On your 28th birthday you receive a grant of $100,000 to be invested or spent entirely at your discretion. Start a business, start a school, get the band working, research something important, pay off some debt. The children of the rich get this already, we are just levelling the playing field.

A parliament of mothers is convened, so that we can listen to their advice.

When you become a mother you get a salary, a house and superannuation. Most traditional cultures looked after mothers better than we do.

A parliament of farmers is convened to terminate the government assault on farmers and allow them to feed us.

A parliament of Exporters is convened so that they can tell us how we should help them to earn the export dollars that pay for our life.

Sin taxes removed on sugar, fags, grog (smokers are sharper every day for 40 years, then die 10 years early, they save 'health' expenditure, drinkers die happy and early again saving money) Did we find that less smoking brings more obesity. Is that factored into their 'calculations'? Does an after work drink help people keep it together? Life choices belong to the individual, not the government. You cannot force us to live a bleak, blinkered, bowdlerised, bounded, life, full of blathered bullshit and bashings any more.

Two Prime Ministers as for Consuls in Ancient Rome (internal, external). Maybe we should call them 'Consuls'.

Six month term for the Prime Ministers, directly elected by ZIT

Party members.

Four deputy Prime Ministers, two previous and two next, directly elected by ZIT Party members.

Press questions directed to the appropriate minister.

The dignity of the Prime Ministerial office to be enabled by disallowing ill-informed, ideological and impertinent questions from the pretend journalists. 'Gotcha' tricks are cynical, pathetic, reprehensible nonsense.

Two Governors General, as for Prime Ministers. Maybe we should call them 'Elders'.

Six month term for Governors General, directly elected by ZIT Party members

Four deputy Governors General, two previous and two next, directly elected by ZIT Party members.

These thoughts offered to demonstrate there are many ideas available for consideration.

It Is Time

Together we can get things moving and make a much better life for the Productive Aussies.

Macron came from nowhere with a new party to takeover France. It can be done.

The voters are ready to move forward, we just need to provide the framework and candidates.

Let's do it.

POLICY CHOICES

Mandatory

Recommendation: Income tax annulled. It is your money, spend it however you wish.

Recommendation: Get the tax man out of the private life of Aussies. It is your life, they have no right to 'gate-crash' your party.

Recommendation: Get regulators off the backs of Aussies. Grovelling to government officials not appropriate. We pay their salary, they should be grovelling to us.

Recommendation: It is your life, chase your dream, do your thing, whatever you choose.

Recommendation: Recognition for Productive Aussies.

Recommendation: Immigration policy review.

Recommendation: Build surge capacity into all systems.

Recommendation: Build triage systems for all services.

Recommendation: Design of induction experiences that will produce useful citizens. No Karens or bludgers.

Recommendation: Electoral misconduct vigorously pursued and eliminated. Mandatory sentence of 12 months for public sector workers who door-knock in their work uniform. You do not deserve to live in Australia. Also a rerun of the perverted election.

Recommendation: Parliament focussed on helping economy grow, delivering health outcomes and citizen benefits, less yapping and name calling.

Recommendation: Question time cancelled.

Recommendation: Dismantle the corrupt superannuation

industry.

For Discussion In Branches

Recommendation: Schooling not compulsory.

Recommendation: New institutions to research Aluminium, Nuclear, Electricity, Rail, Space, Export, Water Management, Power Management.

Recommendation: New institutions to teach Aluminium, Nuclear, Electricity, Rail, Space, Export, Water Management, Power Management.

Recommendation: New institutions to facilitate Aluminium, Nuclear, Electricity, Rail, Space, Export, Water Management, Power Management.

Recommendation: Summit to gain advice from Aluminium, Nuclear, Electricity, Rail, Space, Export, Water Management, Power Management industries.

Recommendation: Initiate space industry projects.

Recommendation: Build dams.

Recommendation: Build nuclear power plants.

Recommendation: Build ports, airports, rail, road.

Recommendation: Commission agriculture research projects to focus on: production issues, funding issues, water issues, quality issues, preserving and packaging issues, exporting and logistics issues. Then do it.

Recommendation: Convene Parliament of Mothers, listen up, then reform the world according to the advice.

Recommendation: 18th birthday company formed for every Aussie.

Recommendation: 28th birthday $100,000 for every Aussie.

Recommendation: Regulations reduced in number and complexity.

Recommendation: Regulator numbers reduced.

Recommendation: The entire health system to be redesigned.

Recommendation: Medical logistics re-imagined.

Recommendation: Medical triage re-imagined.

Recommendation: Medical knowledge available to all citizens.

Recommendation: Processes created to enable legal evolution.

Recommendation: Review law of contract to standardise and simplify. Eliminate cynical dirty tricks like the supermarket company who sought to bypass the restraint of trade law by having a rental contract that reduced their rent to 1% of the normal rent if another supermarket was allowed into the shopping centre. More unconscionable conduct. They should be broken up.

Recommendation: Review dispute resolution seeking rapid informed decisions.

Recommendation: Materials to explain operation of the law for citizens.

Recommendation: Lawyers barred from entering parliament.

Recommendation: The Australian Law Reform Commission be closed.

Recommendation: Spill of all public sector jobs.

Recommendation: Value test for all public sector jobs.

Recommendation: Government advice available everywhere.

Recommendation: Training of backup drivers, nurses and para-medics.

Recommendation: Provide land for farming.

Recommendation: Provide land for housing.

Recommendation: Build massive housing projects on South head, Victoria Barracks and similar locations.

Recommendation: Guarantee low-cost, reliable power to all industries.

Recommendation: Development and distribution of materials designed to help our young understand how a civilised society functions.

Recommendation: Briefing to show that exporters pay for the standard of living we all enjoy.

Recommendation: Simplify systems so that they can be self administering.

How Much Is Enough

Too many, however there is no shortage of ideas. We do not need the greens, the pronoun people or other chintzy chanters.
You choose the priorities.

EPILOGUE

Further Development

We will incorporate in the next edition what we learn from your feedback. We anticipate that there will be more stories of useful Aussies, more thoughts on migration, more industries where we can dominate, more thoughts on how to achieve, fewer and slimmer institutions and more thinking on how to use our democratic processes to set resilient Aussies free.

Contact

feedback: pluckycountry@gmail.com
Support: If you wish to support this program, send $10 to:
Australia BSB: 303111 Account Number: 0711949.

BIBLIOGRAPHY

Acemoglu D., Robinson J. A., (2021), The Narrow Corridor

Acemoglu D., (2012), Why Nations Fail, MIT

Alder K., (1996), Australia's Uranium Opportunities, Pauline M. Alder

Aluminium Industry, https://aluminium.org.au/australian-industry/ viewed 2 August 2021

Applebaum A., (2021) The Atlantic 16/11/2021

Atlas S. W., (2021), A Plague Upon Our House

Beard R., (2021), Sad Little Men

Black, C. (2018). "The Canadian Manifesto", Sutherland House

Black J., (2010), War a Short History

Black J., (2021), Logistics: The Key to Victory,

Blainey G., (1966), The Tyranny of Distance, Sun Books

Blainey G., (2015), The Story of Australia's People Volume I

Blainey G., (2016), The Story of Australia's People Volume II

Bloomfield N., (2017), Almost a French Australia

Bronowski J., (1973), The Ascent of Man, BBC

Cameron-Ash M., (2021), Beating France to Botany Bay

Cater, N., (2013), The Lucky Culture, Harper Collins

Clark G., (2009), A Farewell to Alms

Clark g., (2014), The Son also Rises

Clastres P., (1974), Society Against the State

Covid restrictions, https://spectatorworld.com/topic/dmv-shows-covid-restrictions-never-go-away/ Viewed: 5 October 2021

Davis E., (2021), All Pathology, All the Time

What ails a culture that sees illness everywhere? https://www.thenewatlantis.com/publications/all-pathology-all-the-time

Davis E., (2020), Chemically Imbalanced, University of Chicago Press

Davison, G. (1993) The Unforgiving Minute. How Australians Learned to Tell the Time, Melbourne University Press, Melbourne

Deutsch, D., (2012), The Beginning of Infinity

Devine T. M., (2018), The Scottish Clearances, Allen Lane

Dickens, C., (1853) Bleak House

Eco U., (2020), How to spot a Fascist

Ferguson, Niall., The Great Degeneration, Penguin Books Ltd. Kindle Edition

Ferguson, Niall., (2004), Empire

Ferguson, Niall., (2016), The Square and Tower

Ferguson, Niall., (2021), Doom

Ferguson, Niall., (2012), Civilisation

Ferguson, Niall., https://www.bloomberg.com/opinion/articles/2021-11-08/niall-ferguson-america-s-woke-universities-need-to-be-replaced viewed 9 November 2021

Furedi F. (2004), Therapy Culture, Pluto

Gall J., (1975), Systemantics, Simon and Schuster

Garratt B., (1996), The Fish Rots from the Head, Profile Books

Gibson M., (1995), Braveheart

Graeber D., (2014), Debt

Graeber D., Wengrow D., (2021), the Dawn of Everything

Grant R. W., (1966), The Incredible Bread Machine

Greer G., (2008), On Rage

Greer G., (1990), The madwoman's underclothes

Gurri M., (2014), The Revolt of the Public

Hardman I., (2021), Why we get the Wrong Politicians

Henrich, J., (2010), The WEIRDest People in the World

Hinton L., (2018), The Bootle Boy, Scribe

Horne, D., (1964), Lucky Country, Penguin

HOWARD, P. K., (2009), Life Without Lawyers: Restoring

Responsibility in America. New York: Norton & Company

Huxley A., (1932), Brave new World

Kahneman D., Sibony O., Sunstein C. R., (2021), Noise

Kemp D., (2018), The Land of Dreams, The Miegunyah Press

Kemp D., (2019), A Free Country, The Miegunyah Press

Kemp D., (2019), A Democratic Nation, The Miegunyah Press

Kemp D., (2021), A Liberal State, The Miegunyah Press

Kieza G., (2021), Macquarie

Kieza G., (2020), Banks

King A., (2013), The Blunders of Our Governments

Legal Services, https://www.quicksprout.com/best-online-legal-services/ viewed: 11/10/2021

Letts Q., (2021), Stop Bloody Bossing Me About

Linnell G., (2020), Buckley's Chance

Lomborg B., (2003), The skeptical environmentalist: measuring the real state of the world, Cambridge University Press

Lomborg B., (2004), Global crises, global solutions, Cambridge University Press

Lomborg B., (2010), Smart solutions to climate change: Comparing costs and benefits, Cambridge University Press

Lomborg B., (2020), False Alarm: How Climate Change Panic Costs Us Trillions, Hurts the Poor, and Fails to Fix the Planet Hachette UK

McLachlan I., (2001), The Hiking Politician, Seaview Press

McKenna M., (2012), From the Edge

Madoyan g., (2016), Gramscian Hegemony

Maine H., (1861), Ancient Law

Marx, K., Engels, F., (1847), Manifesto of the Communist Party and its genesis Published by the Marxists Internet Archive

Marshall Alexandra, Twitter @ellymelly

Menzies, R., (1942), The Forgotten People - a speech by Robert Menzies

Mercola, J., Cummins, R., (2021), The Truth About COVID-19, Chelsea Green Publishing

Morgan E., (1972), The Descent of Woman, Stein and Day NYC

Orwell G., (1949), 1984

Otte T. G., (2020), Statesmen of Europe

Parkinson C. N., (1957), Parkinson's Law

Pascoe B., (2014), Dark Emu

Paul R., https://libertytree.com/randpaul/1391 14/10/2021

Peters T., Waterman R., (1982), In Search of Excellence

Pierce, J. L., Inside the Mason Court Revolution: The High Court of Australia, Transformed (Durham: Carolina Academic Press, 2006) pages vii–x, 3–334, ISBN 159460 061 9.

Plimer I., (2014), Not for greens: he who sups with the Devil should have a long spoon, Connor Court Pub.

Popper, Karl, (1945), The Open Society and Its Enemies, Routledge

Pringle J. M, Molnar G., (1959), Australian Accent

Reagan R., (1982), source America by Heart (2010), Palin S.

Rosling H., Rosling O., Roanlund A., (2018), Factfulness

Russell, B. (1915). "The ethics of war.", International Journal of Ethics, Volume 25 No. 2

Scott J. C., (1998), Seeing Like a State

Scott J. C., (2017), Against the Grain

Shaw, G.B.S., (1906), The Doctor's Dilemma

Shakespeare, W. (1992). Macbeth. Wordsworth Editions

Slingerland E., (2021), Drunk

Solzhenitsyn, A., (1917) The Red Wheel, Node III, Book 1, University of Notre Dame Press

Stripper Image, https://portal.engineersaustralia.org.au/heritage/ridley-stripper-first-mechanical-grain-harvester-1843.

Sutton P., Walshe K., Farmers or Hunter Gatherers?

Taleb N. N., (2018), Skin in the Game

Taleb N. N., (2012), Antifragile

Tocqueville A. de., (1862), Democracy in America, Translator – Henry Reeve, A Penn State Electronic Classics Series Publication

Tolstoy, L. (1995). Anna Karenina (A. Maude & L. Maude, Trans.). Wordsworth Editions

Turchin P., Hoyer D., (2020), Figuring Out The Past

Turchin P., (2007), War and Peace and War

Ultraviolet Light Fights New Virus
https://www.ncbi.nlm.nih.gov/pmc/articles/PMC7319933/
University of Austin.
https://www.bloomberg.com/opinion/articles/2021-11-08/
niall-ferguson-america-s-woke-universities-need-to-be-
replaced viewed 9 November 2021
Vort-Ronald P., (1973), A Culture of Illich, Australian Left Review
Wilson, E. O., (2012), The Social Conquest of Earth (p. 61). Liveright. Kindle Edition

ABOUT THE AUTHOR

Geoff Stewart

A lifetime of observing, discussing and pondering the human condition.
Plus, Charirman of the Victorian Branch of the Australian Computer Society, Fellow of the Institute of Directors, Fellow of CEDA, convenor of MBA program, Lecturer in Strategy and Marketing.
Family, 5 children, 6 grandchildren.

BOOKS BY THIS AUTHOR

Sail South Till The Butter Melts

Atlantic voyage in an open boat. Plus some biographical bits.